A Place of
Quiet Rest

A Place of Quiet Rest

FINDING INTIMACY WITH
GOD THROUGH A DAILY
DEVOTIONAL LIFE

Nancy Leigh
DeMoss

MOODY PUBLISHERS
CHICAGO

All Scripture quotations, unless indicated, are taken from the *Holy Bible: New International Version*®. NIV®. Copyright © 1973, 1978, 1984 by International Bible Society. Used by permission of Zondervan Publishing House. All rights reserved.

Scripture quotations designated (KJV) are from the *King James Version*.

Scripture quotations designated (TLB) are from *The Living Bible*, © 1971 by Tyndale House Publishers, Wheaton, IL.

Cover Design: Ragont Design

ISBN: 978-0-8024-6643-3

We hope you enjoy this book from Moody Publishers. Our goal is to provide high-quality, thought-provoking books and products that connect truth to your real needs and challenges. For more information on other books and products written and produced from a biblical perspective, go to www.moodypublishers.com or write to:

Moody Publishers
820 N. LaSalle Boulevard
Chicago, IL 60610

15 17 19 20 18 16 14

Printed in the United States of America

To my Beloved Lord Jesus.
You are "the chiefest among ten thousand"
and "altogether lovely."

"The companions hearken to Thy voice:
cause me to hear it."

Jesus, Thou Joy of loving hearts,
Thou Fount of life, Thou Light of men,
From the best bliss that earth imparts,
We turn unfilled to Thee again.

We taste Thee, O Thou living Bread,
And long to feast upon Thee still;
We drink of Thee, the Fountainhead,
And thirst our souls from Thee to fill.

BERNARD OF CLAIRVAUX

CONTENTS

SECTION 2: Responding to His Word

Mary . . . anointed the feet of Jesus.

PART 6
The Product of a Devotional Life

*Let my beloved come into his garden
and eat his pleasant fruits.*

From the Heart of . . .

OREWORD
Before You Begin . . .

*D*evotion to the Lord Jesus. We all desire it.

When it comes to drawing close to God, every Christian wants to be plunged under the waterfall of His joy. We want to get our hearts beating in rhythm with His. If we're sad, we want His smile. If we're lost, we want Him to find us. "Lord, embrace me with a passion that seizes and melts me into a union with You that can never be broken. Part the heavens and come down," we pray; "throw open the door of my heart and take possession."

Our Christian instincts call for this. It's getting there that's the struggle.

How do we get started? Flip open the Bible and "let the Spirit lead"? Study a topic? Memorize a chapter? Surround ourselves with commentaries and Bible dictionaries? (We want to do this right!) A carefully structured quiet time with the Lord is good, but a growing life of devotion to the Savior is more—much more—than "Do A, B, or C and you will know Him better."

Personal relationships don't work that way, certainly not when it comes to God. If we want to grow closer to someone—God or anybody—it means pressing hearts together. Learning how to communicate. Finding joy in each other. Searching out the other's soul. A strong relationship is the weaving together of many shared experiences, some of which are serendipitous and off-the-cuff, others of which are structured and well-defined. Such things make for intimacy. Disciplining ourselves to spend regular time with someone, even with God, can be regulated, but not the intimacy itself.

A Place of Quiet Rest is a guide into that intimacy. Rather than a how-to book, Nancy Leigh DeMoss provides for you an excellent road map: a guide using Scripture and hymns, testimonies, poems, counsel, and wisdom to help you know God and be known. *A Place of Quiet Rest* is anything but a mechanistic approach to cultivating a devotional life with the Lord Jesus; it is a gentle yet clear nudge on every page, a pointing-in-the-right-direction in every chapter. It is a book which will help you encounter God as you push past the regimen to the place where you can embrace the Savior in a natural—no, a *supernatural* way.

And what will happen when you, in turn, embrace God with a passion that seizes and melts you into sweet union with Him? How will you be affected as you follow the guides in *A Place of Quiet Rest?* As a saint of old once said, your joy will be fervent but not feverish. You will be energetic but not excitable. You will be speedy in doing things, but not hasty. Prudent, but not selfish. Resolute and fearless, but not rash. You will have joy without a lot of parade and noise. Your soul will be serene, yet people all around you will feel the influence of God.

It's what devotion to Jesus looks like on you.

Want it? Rather, do you want *Him?* You hold in your hands a splendid guide.

JONI EARECKSON TADA

ACKNOWLEDGMENTS

*M*y friends will tell you that when I am in the midst of a writing project, I sometimes can be heard to moan, "I'm in labor!"

Although I have never given birth to a physical baby, I have been blessed on two occasions to stand by and encourage a friend through the difficult, but rewarding, process of childbirth.

I don't know how much real help I was to my friend. But I do know that the lengthy process of "giving birth" to this book has been significantly eased by the encouragement and assistance of many friends and coworkers who have been there by my side.

Jim Bell and the editorial team at Moody Press—Shortly after the Lord nudged my heart to begin writing (which I was reluctant to do), you came along and urged me to do so. I am grateful for your heart to get this message out.

Carolyn Nystrom—You are a wonderful coach. I have learned much from you. Thank you for your honest input that made this a better book, and for your kind spirit that made it a joy to work together.

Mike, Becca, Monica, Sandra, Gayle, and Stephen—What an incredible staff team you are! You lighten my load in so many ways; you have prayed, served, and given tirelessly so I could focus on this task with a minimum of distractions.

The leadership team of Life Action Ministries—You released me to write and took many of my responsibilities on your own shoulders to make it possible. For more than twenty years we have labored together in His vineyard. Your lives have molded mine more than you will ever know. I love serving Him with you!

My dear praying friends—How blessed I am to have you. I am constantly amazed at the way you stand by me and hold up my hands in the midst of the battle. I can't imagine how I could ever make it without the covering and protection of your prayers.

To each of you, I express a deep sense of debt and gratitude. Thank you for being there through the "labor and delivery." We have birthed this book together.

Now we give it back to You, Lord Jesus, with the prayer that You will use it to bless Your people and make them fruitful.

This is not a book written by an expert.

Rather, it is written by a woman in process—a woman on a pilgrimage to know God.

For me, that pilgrimage began months before I was born, as my parents dedicated me to the Lord and purposed to teach me (and the six children that would follow) the Word and ways of God.

Much as a greenhouse is designed to nurture young plants and protect them from influences that might damage their tender roots, the climate of our home was carefully controlled to minimize influences that could possibly be unwholesome (we did not own a television or take a paper, for example) and to provide constant nurture in the Word of God.

The Spirit used the spiritual care of those earliest years to cultivate the soil of my heart, to make it tender and responsive to His wooing and to make me aware of my need for a Savior. My first conscious memory is the afternoon of May 14, 1963, when, at the age of four, I gave my heart to Christ. Although I didn't realize it at the time, I understand now that at that moment, God planted within me a seed—the seed of eternal life. He placed within me a new life—the life of His Son, Jesus. That life is eternal. It is supernatural.

And that was only the beginning. God's intent, determined in eternity past, was that that seed should be carefully nurtured, that it should take root and produce fruit—and that one day that seed would produce a woman who would bear the likeness of His dear Son and who would reproduce others after the same likeness.

Until that day in 1963, according to God's Word, I was "dead in trespasses and sin"—I had no connection to the God of the universe. But at that moment, through repentance and faith in Jesus Christ, I became alive. And with that new birth came evidence of life.

It's not hard to tell that a newborn baby is alive—he breathes, his heart beats, he gets hungry and thirsty, he grows, he communicates, he cries. And so, my spiritual birth was accompanied by signs of spiritual life—a capacity and a longing to know God, a heart that beats and cries after God.

I cannot take any credit for what took place that day. At the time, I had no idea of all that God had gone through to draw my heart to Himself and to make it possible for me to enter into an eternal relationship with Him. I had little comprehension of the fact that God is the supreme Lover who desires intimacy with His creatures. And I certainly had little awareness of the incredible price He had paid to make it possible for me to live in union and communion with Him.

All I knew was that I needed Him, that He wanted me, and that Jesus was the One who made it possible for us to have that relationship.

Now, looking back, I can see that what took place that day was the starting point of a relationship—a longing in my heart, corresponding to the longing in His heart, to know Him, to walk with Him, to be intimate with Him, to enjoy fellowship with Him, and to share our lives together in an eternal love relationship.

Early in my Christian life, I learned about one of the most essential ingredients in nurturing that relationship with God, as I became aware that my father began each day with a practice that he called "devotions."

A businessman with many demands on his time, and active in ministry of many kinds, my father was not one to spend time frivolously. Yet somehow, in the midst of an extremely active and busy household, and with incessant demands of travel and meetings, there was one constant in his life—he never got started into the business of the day without first having spent an hour or more alone with the Lord.

I don't recall ever actually being with him during those times—though I did frequently see him reading his Bible—but somehow we all knew that this time in the Word and prayer was more important to him than any other activity of his day. As I got older, I learned something of how this had come to be such an indispensable part of his life.

During his teenage and young adult years, in search of thrills, my father became addicted to gambling, adopting a freewheeling lifestyle that kept him moving from one gambling hot spot to another, destroyed any sense of values he may have had, and caused no little heartache to his parents. He was not looking for God—the Scripture indicates that there is no one who seeks after God—but the "Hound of Heaven" was pursuing him. One night, while in his midtwenties, having made a mess of his life, he came under the preaching of the gospel. He was converted and never looked back.

Early in his Christian life, he was challenged to give the first part of every day to the Lord in the Word and in prayer. From that day until the day he went to heaven twenty-eight years later, *he never missed one single day* of this devotional practice. Nothing was more important to him than cultivating his relationship with the Lord, and he believed strongly that nothing was more essential to maintaining that relationship than a daily time alone with the Lord in the Word and prayer.

Daily devotions was not something my parents forced on us, but the influence of my dad's example and training in this area was profound. Although he has been with the Lord since 1979, the image of a dad on his knees before the Lord (I don't know how many kneeling pads he wore out over the years) is indelibly etched on my mind and in my heart.

I want to be quick to say that my own record in this matter is far from my dad's. Although I have made a practice since earliest childhood of beginning my day with the Lord, I have to acknowledge that this is a discipline that has never come easily for me. As much as I cherish and value and need this time with the Lord, to this day I find myself having to fight to make it a consistent reality.

I battle my flesh, which loves to sleep, is easily distracted, and does not like to sit still and be quiet. I battle my schedule with its never-ending "to do" list. I battle interruptions—many of my own making.

There are many mornings when I have allowed the pillow, the phone, or piles of office work to win out, and have ended up spending only a few hurried moments with Him. On occasion, I have even missed out altogether on spending any time alone with Him.

But over the years I have come to believe with all my heart that this is something worth fighting for. I have come to understand that one of the reasons it is such a battle is that the Enemy of my soul knows if he can defeat me here, he will ultimately be able to defeat me in every other area of my spiritual life.

Satan hates God, and he works tirelessly to convince Christians that they can operate on their own, independently of God. If we concede the battle to him, he knows that we will end up defeated, frustrated, barren, and useless to God. Worse, we will end up doubting God, despairing of His goodness, in bondage to our flesh, and resisting His will.

In more recent years, I have discovered another, even more important, reason for pressing on to protect this time alone with the Lord. I have come to see that "devotions" is not so much an obligation of the Christian life, as it is an incredible opportunity to know the God of the universe. He has issued to you and to me an invitation to draw near to Him, to walk right into the "Holy of Holies" to enter into an intimate love relationship with Him.

"Devotions" has become for me, not so much a *duty* (although there are still days when it is just that), as a *delight*—an awesome privilege to share sweet union and communion with the Bridegroom of my soul.

I am convinced that few subjects evoke such feelings of guilt, failure, and frustration among believers as the matter of "daily devotions." Having talked with and listened to thousands of women across the country, I believe there is within most Christian women a feeling that "I ought to be more faithful and consistent in this area."

Of those women who do have some sort of devotional life, many—perhaps a majority—approach this time with a sense of duty. Others have tried and failed so many times they are tempted to give up—some already have. Still others have never even got started and have no idea what they are missing.

Then there are those women whose lives bear the sweet, rich fruit of meeting with God on a consistent basis. I have been drawn to a number of these women over the years. The fragrance of their lives has deepened my own longing to know God. (In each chapter of this book, one of those women will share something of her own experience in cultivating a daily devotional life.)

Wherever God finds you, if you are His child, I believe there is within you something that will never be satisfied with anything less than intimate fellowship with your Creator, Redeemer, and heavenly Father. Until you see Him face-to-face, you will never cease to hunger and thirst to know Him more. I know that longing deep within my own soul.

Jesus said, "If anyone is thirsty, let him come to me and drink" (John 7:37). This is a book for thirsty souls. It is an invitation to come to *Him*—not to another program, another thing to add to your "to do" list, another requirement—but to Jesus, the Source of all Life. Come to Him and drink. Drink deeply; keep on drinking; let Him quench your thirst; and then watch as rivers of living water flow out through you to quench the thirst of those around you.

NANCY LEIGH DEMOSS

PART ONE

The Priority
of a
Devotional Life

One thing have I desired of the Lord, that will I seek after.

PSALM 27:4 KJV

The more I think of and pray about the state of religion in this country, and all over the world, the deeper my conviction becomes that the low state of the spiritual life of Christians is due to the fact that they do not realize that the aim and object of conversion is to bring the soul even here on earth to a daily fellowship with the Father in heaven.

When once this truth has been accepted, the believer will perceive how indispensable it is to the spiritual life of a Christian to take time each day with God's Word, and in prayer to wait upon God for His presence and love to be revealed.

ANDREW MURRAY

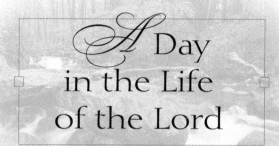

CHAPTER 1

A Day in the Life of the Lord

Some time ago, I asked the women who were attending a weekend conference where I was speaking to write on a three-by-five-inch card why they had come and what it was they were hoping God would do in their lives through the weekend. "Where does God find you as we start this weekend?" I asked.

Later, as I read the responses to my question, I was amazed at how many of them sounded alike. Here is a sampling of what those women expressed:

"I feel I'm out of control sometimes with so many pressures."

"I face too much stress and responsibility."

"I need God to show me how to cope with the stresses at this moment."

"I feel like I'm torn in all directions. I want God to show me how to manage my different 'hats' of teacher, mother, wife, and daughter successfully, and still have time for church work and 'me.'"

"I need to stop worrying about everything. I try not to and I know I shouldn't, but my worries that I conjure up even disturb my sleep and dreams."

"I've given myself up to service for about twenty-four months, and I feel a need to slow myself down and renew myself, but life gets real hectic."

"With a new baby, I need to find the Lord's peace and rest—physically and emotionally."

"I often get overly busy and find my day gone without having done the things I most wanted to do."

"I am a single person by divorce, and I really am tired."

"I've left a whirlwind at home, and need a renewed spirit to face all that these coming weeks will hold."

"I want to slow down. I feel as if I'm on a speeding treadmill, and if I try to jump off I will stumble and fall."

"I need help with my frazzled, frenzied state."

"My busyness has robbed me of my joy."

Do you find yourself relating to any of these feelings? I find these kinds of responses are increasingly common among the women I meet. Why do we live such hectic, harried lives? Is this what God intended for us? And can we actually get off that speeding treadmill without hurting ourselves (and others) in the process?

Busy Days

The first chapter of the gospel of Mark gives us a glimpse into a day in the life of the Lord Jesus. In some respects, this particular day was not unlike many of the days that you and I experience.

We pick up the account in verse 21:

They went to Capernaum, and when the Sabbath came, Jesus went into the synagogue and began to teach. The people were amazed at his teaching, because he taught them as one who had authority, not as the teachers of the law. (MARK 1:21–22)

If you've ever taught a Sunday school class, led a small group, or taught a Bible study, you know there's a lot more behind these words than what appears on the surface.

You know that you don't just get up before a group and teach the Word of God with power and effectiveness apart from a lot of time spent in preparation—not just preparation of the notes and the material, but preparation of your heart and life.

I love teaching the Scripture; to me there is nothing quite like seeing the Word of God penetrate and transform lives. But the process of preparing to speak is an intense one for me.

I agonize to determine what it is that the Lord wants me to teach; I wrestle with the passages involved, seeking to understand what the Scripture really means; I labor to put the material together in a form that is understandable and meaningful to the listener.

Throughout the process, I ask the Holy Spirit to search my own heart, to shine the light of His Word into every nook and cranny of my life, and to show me where I don't measure up to the truth I am about to proclaim. Before opening my mouth to speak, I spend time in prayer, pleading with God for a fresh anointing of His Spirit on my life and my lips, and interceding for those who will hear the message. I feel like a runner about to run an important race—every muscle taut, totally concentrated on the race ahead.

Then, while I'm actually teaching, there is more energy expended—physically, mentally, emotionally, and spiritually. I am intensely focused, never letting up from my goal—I want the truth to penetrate every heart; I want every individual to say yes to God about any issue He is addressing in her life.

When I have finished speaking, the battle is still not over—that is when the Enemy often seeks to discourage me with feelings of inadequacy or to tempt me with seeking the praise of men for my ministry. By the time it's all over, I am generally depleted and in need of restoration.

So when I read that Jesus began this particular day by

teaching in the synagogue, I know this was not just a casual effort on His part. The people listened attentively to Him because they could tell this was not your normal, run-of-the-mill Sabbath message. Unlike the preachers they were accustomed to hearing, Jesus spoke with authority and power. We know that in order for this to be possible, He had spent concentrated time with His heavenly Father in preparation. As He ministered, He was being expended on behalf of others.

The apostle Paul said, "I will very gladly spend and be spent for you" (2 Corinthians 12:15 KJV). That's part of what is involved in ministering to others, whether in a synagogue, a Sunday school class, or a house full of little ones.

Confronting Evil

This was just the beginning of Jesus' day—His work was not nearly over. Before He even had a chance to finish His message, there was an interruption in the service. Let's continue reading in Mark 1:

> Just then a man in their synagogue who was possessed by an evil spirit cried out, "What do you want with us, Jesus of Nazareth? Have you come to destroy us? I know who you are—the Holy One of God!"
>
> "Be quiet!" said Jesus sternly. "Come out of him!" The evil spirit shook the man violently and came out of him with a shriek.
>
> The people were all so amazed that they asked each other, "What is this? A new teaching—and with authority! He even gives orders to evil spirits and they obey him." (MARK 1:23–27)

Here we see Jesus engaged in a battle between heaven and hell. Everywhere Jesus went during His years of earthly ministry, the demons of hell were stirred up because He lived and spoke and ministered in the power and the authority of God.

Obviously, this was not some casual, relaxed encounter with the Enemy. This was all-out warfare.

Now, I have never exorcised a demon. And in the course of

an average day, you and I are not likely to have audible or visible encounters with demons. But God's Word teaches that we are in the midst of a battle against "principalities and powers"—that at this very moment there is a cosmic warfare being waged between heaven and hell. And sometimes, God sends us right into the front lines of that battle. Many of the people we encounter and deal with on a daily basis are in the midst of an intense spiritual battle for their souls, and sometimes we get caught in the cross fire.

In the course of being a wife, a mother, a daughter, a friend, an employee, you will find yourself in the midst of difficult, strenuous, demanding situations where you have to be alert to the schemes of Satan and skilled in using the sword of the Spirit to fight off his attacks. There is a natural drain that is a part of being God's servant in these situations. Jesus experienced those moments of intense confrontation with the powers of darkness.

As a result of this encounter with the demonized man, the Scripture tells us that "news about [Jesus] spread quickly over the whole region of Galilee" (v. 28). Try to imagine how that must have complicated Jesus' life. All of a sudden, people all over the area wanted Him to come speak at their synagogues and banquets, wanted to interview Him for their publications, wanted Him to heal their sick and cast out their demons. They all wanted a piece of Him. Later in this passage we learn that the time finally came when Jesus couldn't even stay in the cities, but had to find quiet, remote places where the crowds couldn't find Him, in order to get time alone with His Father.

Perhaps you have had the experience of ministering to someone in need—lending a listening ear to a discouraged young mother, helping out in your child's classroom, preparing a meal for a family in a crisis, being a youth sponsor on a mission trip, ministering to a friend's troubled teenager, or offering biblical counsel to a woman in a shaky marriage. Then the word spreads that you are available to help people in need—and all of a sudden, your phone is ringing off the hook with people wanting your time and help.

Everybody Needs Me!

Well, the service at the synagogue is finally over and we feel a sense of relief when we read the next verse: "As soon as they left the synagogue, they went with James and John to the home of Simon and Andrew" (v. 29).

Whew! Jesus has spent hours giving out and expending Himself for others. Finally He has a chance to get away with His friends, away from all the needy people. He gets to go home, kick up His feet, open up a good book, and relax—maybe even take a nap. Right? Wrong!

Read on: "Simon's mother-in-law was in bed with a fever, and they told Jesus about her" (v. 30). Jesus is finally out of the public eye, back in the safe haven of a friend's home, and even there, someone needs Him.

Do you relate to any of this as a woman? Do you ever feel that there is no time, no place where you can totally escape the demands of other people? If it's not the people at work, it's your husband; if it's not your husband, it's your children; if it's not your children, it's the neighbor's children; if it's not someone else's children, it's your mother-in-law; if it's not your mother-in-law, it's . . .

But as we would expect, the serving heart of Jesus comes out and He makes Himself available to meet the need: "So he went to her, took her hand and helped her up. The fever left her and she began to wait on them" (v. 31).

Finally, Jesus can close the door and settle in for a nice quiet evening alone with his friends . . . "Martha, go see who's knocking at the door!"

> That evening after sunset the people brought to Jesus all the sick and demon-possessed. The whole town gathered at the door. (MARK 1:32–33)

I don't know how many people came to see Jesus that

evening, but it sounds like a lot to me! Remember, this is still the same day—He started early that morning, teaching, casting out demons, and healing the sick, and now the whole city is lined up at His door wanting help.

Do you ever feel like the whole town is gathered at your door? Maybe it's your bathroom door, and you're just trying to get three minutes alone without having to answer any questions—but somebody's knocking on the door, the doorbell is ringing, the phone is ringing, the oven timer is buzzing, your three children seem like thirty-three, you feel like half the world is sick, and everybody needs you—all at the same time. You panic: "There's just not enough of me to go around!"

And Jesus healed many who had various diseases. He also drove out many demons. (MARK 1:34)

How Did He Do It?

You wonder, How did He do it? How did He stay sane? How did He keep His sense of equilibrium? How did He keep meeting the needs of so many people without falling apart Himself?

We know Jesus was God. But He was also a man—He got tired; He got hungry; He knew what it was to have crowds pressing around Him all the time; He knew what it was to have His privacy invaded. But He kept right on letting the crowds into His life. He kept on teaching, healing, confronting the powers of hell—and never a cross or impatient word. How did He do it?

Besides, He was only given three years on this earth to accomplish the whole eternal plan of redemption. Talk about a long "to do" list! Yet He never seemed hurried, harried, or overwhelmed with all there was to do in a day. Why not? How did He handle all the stress, strain, and responsibility without "losing it"?

I believe verse 35 gives us the key—not only to Jesus' life, but also to your life and mine, whatever our specific responsibilities and circumstances may be. That verse begins, *"Very early in the morning . . ."*

I don't know about you—but when I've had a long, draining day like the one we just read about, I know exactly what I want to do very early the next morning. *Nothing—except sleep!*

Now, there's nothing wrong with sleeping when our bodies need it. But Jesus knew there was something He needed that next morning even more desperately than His body needed sleep. He had poured Himself out for countless needy individuals, and His spirit needed to be replenished. He knew it would never happen once the crowd woke up, so what did He do?

"Very early in the morning, while it was still dark, Jesus got up . . ." He got up! The Scripture says that Jesus was tempted in every point as we are; so I have no doubt that Jesus was tempted to sleep in. But He made a choice to say no to His body and yes to His Father. He got up. Then He "left the house and went off to a solitary place, where he prayed" (v. 35).

And He did so none too soon. For it wasn't long before "Simon and his companions went to look for him, and when they found him, they exclaimed: 'Everyone is looking for you!'" (vv. 36–37).

However, having just been in touch with His heavenly Father, Jesus knew exactly how He was to respond to the demands of the new day: "Jesus replied, 'Let us go somewhere else—to the nearby villages—so I can preach there also. That is why I have come'" (v. 38).

Why was this morning appointment with His Father so crucial to Jesus' earthly ministry among us?

Jesus knew that any power or ability He had to minister to others was due to the fact that He was "one with the Father." He knew it was essential for Him to stay connected to His Father, for that was His Source of life, joy, power, peace, and fruitfulness. He knew He had to walk in union and communion with His Father if He was to know and do His Father's will. He had no other purpose for being on this earth than to do the will of His Father. So He had no higher priority than to abide in intimate, unbroken fellowship with His Father, so that He might fulfill His Father's will.

For Jesus, time alone with God was not an option. It was not something He tacked on to an overcrowded schedule. It was His lifeline to the Father. It was not something He could do without. It was the highest priority of His life—more important than being with His disciples, more important than preaching the gospel, more important than time with His mother and brothers, more important than responding to the demands and needs of the crowds, more important than anything else.

The gospel of Luke tells us that "Jesus often withdrew to lonely places and prayed" (Luke 5:16). This was the pattern of His life. This is where He got His "marching orders" for the day. This is where He discovered the will of God for His life. This is where He got renewed and restored when virtue had gone out of Him as He ministered to the crowds. This is where He gained the resources to do battle against Satan—and win! This is where He stepped back from the corruption, clutter, and clamor of life on this earth and was given the ability to see the world from God's point of view. This is where He received grace to love the unlovable and power to do the impossible.

And this is precisely where you and I so often miss out on all that God has for us. Unlike Jesus, we attempt to live life in our own energy. We think we can keep giving out without getting replenished. Then, wearied and weakened by the demands of life and ministry, we become impatient and annoyed with the very ones God has sent us to serve. Rather than exhibiting a gracious, calm, joyous spirit, we become uptight, frazzled, and frenzied women, resenting, rather than welcoming, the people and opportunities God brings into our lives.

Is it really possible for us to manifest the same spirit Jesus did when facing pressure? That all depends on whether we are willing to make the same choice He made, to adopt His number one priority as the number one priority of our lives:

Very early in the morning, while it was still dark, Jesus got up, left the house and went off to a solitary place, where he prayed. (MARK 1:35)

MAKING IT PERSONAL

1. Take stock of the usual quantity and quality of time you spend alone with God in the Word, praise, and prayer. Which of the following best describes the current condition of your personal devotional life?

   _____ *For all practical purposes, I have no devotional life.*

   _____ *My devotional life is inconsistent and sporadic.*

   _____ *I am spending time in the Word and prayer on a consistent basis, but I often feel that I am just going through the motions. My devotions are more a matter of duty than delight.*

   _____ *I am meeting alone with the Lord on a daily basis and am cultivating a meaningful, intimate relationship with Him through His Word, prayer, and praise.*

2. Write three or four words that would typically describe your spirit when your schedule is full or you are in the midst of pressured circumstances (for example: calm, prayerful, frenzied, demanding).

3. Based on the account we have just considered in Mark 1, write a brief paragraph describing the way Jesus responded to pressure.

   What do you think accounted for His ability to respond to interruptions, demands, and the incessant needs of those around Him?

4. Take a few moments to pray and ask God to speak to you through this study. Ask Him to make you like Jesus in your response to the circumstances of life. Ask Him to give you a deeper desire to make your relationship with Him the most important priority of your life.

□□□ FROM THE HEART OF □□□
Elisabeth Elliot

We "need Him every hour." If we aim to be consistent in the way we live and walk, we cannot settle for a hit-or-miss nod in God's direction. There is no way to live the Christian life without strong effort, faithful commitment, and spiritual disciplines.

The primary obstacle I face is myself—my laziness, preoccupations, worries, lack of concentration. I must deal with these in the strength of the Lord. But I am responsible to do what I am meant to do. He will help me, but He will not physically move me to the quiet place or to my knees.

Married or single, mothers or not, we must arrange to be quiet, alone, consistently, before God. We must arrange this. We can. "The Lord GOD will help me; therefore shall I not be confounded: therefore have I set my face like a flint, and I know that I shall not be ashamed" (Isaiah 50:7 KJV).

The daily quiet time is an offering up to God of one's praise and all that the day may hold. To start my quiet time, I use an ancient hymn, the *Te Deum*. This begins the day with praise, not with my own petty little lists of what I want.

Then I read the Word, asking the Holy Spirit to apply it to my heart and life.

I sing and memorize psalms and hymns. I seek to make myself, my hopes and fears, the whole of my life (circumstances, duties, work, sorrows and joys, my body) a daily offering and sacrifice, full of thanksgiving.

Throughout the day, I offer up prayer, keeping lists of people and things to pray for. I pray that God will teach me to pray. I use the Lord's Prayer and the prayers of the Epistles to help me pray. There are no legitimate excuses for skipping prayer—prayer can be made, as Brother Lawrence learned, even while scrubbing pots in a kitchen in the monastery.

The older I get, the more I am aware of my desperate need of Christ Himself. I want to listen and learn and glorify Him.

Elisabeth Elliot is a much-loved speaker and author. While she and her first husband, Jim, were young missionaries in Ecuador, her husband was martyred by the Auca Indians. Elisabeth has one daughter, eight grandchildren, and four step-grandchildren, and is married to Lars Gren.

NOTE

Part page: Andrew Murray, *The Secret of Fellowship* (Fort Washington, Pa.: Christian Literature Crusade, 1981), Introduction.

CHAPTER 2

Made
for Intimacy

Everyone loves a love story. Love stories are the stuff that movies and best-sellers and headlines are made of. That's because we were made to give and receive love. We were made for intimacy.

Yet most of us know more about the absence of intimacy than the reality. That sense of aloneness and isolation we have all experienced somewhere in the core of our being is a God-created hole that cries out to be filled; it is a longing for intimacy.

From earliest childhood, we have sought to fill that vacuum—we crave closeness, warmth, and affection; we long to know that we matter to someone, that someone cares, that someone who really knows us still loves us. However, even in the best of families and human relationships, the most we are able to do is somewhat dull the sense of longing; other humans can never completely fill the hole.

That's because the God who created that hole in our hearts is also the only One who can fill it. In the Scriptures we encounter a God who moves toward us, who seeks to draw us to Himself, who knows us intimately and passionately, and who invites us to know Him in the same way.

In the first pages of the book of Genesis, we are introduced to this God who initiates relationship with man. Of all God's creation, man alone is given the capacity to respond to God's initiative, to love Him in return, to know Him, and to enjoy His companionship.

However, no sooner has the story begun than man rejects God's initiative, and intimacy is broken. In response, this Lover-God immediately sets into motion a plan whereby His estranged loved ones may be restored to intimate fellowship with Himself. And what is the outcome of that plan?

When we come to the final pages of Revelation, we see the ultimate fulfillment of the eternal purposes of God, as heaven is peopled with those whose hearts have been won by His love and who will spend eternity in an intimate love relationship with their Creator.

So you see, from start to finish, the Word of God is one incredible love story. And, wonder of wonders, it is a story that has your name and mine in it. Whether you grew up, as I did, in the church, or have no church background at all; whether you have a "respectable" background or a questionable one; whether you are well-versed in the Bible or have only recently opened it for the first time—there is room in this love story for you.

Many of the men and women of Scripture illustrate what it is to be loved by God and to respond to His divine initiative with wonder, worship, and glad surrender.

Those who drank from the deep wells of that divine love longed to linger in His presence and counted it their highest privilege and aim to live in unbroken union and communion with Him. Their lives make us thirsty for intimacy with the Creator-Lover who corresponds to that hole in our hearts.

Adam and Eve: Alone with Their Creator

Adam and Eve were the first of God's creatures to experience this remarkable union. Nowhere do we read of God's conversing with the trees, the fish, or the oceans. Nowhere do we see God seeking out a relationship with any of His creation so far beneath Him—except for man, created in His own image.

Only to Adam and Eve did God reveal Himself, His character, His wishes, His ways. The pair responded to the divine initiative in wonder, love, and obedience. There was no fear, for there was perfect love between God and His loved ones. There was no shame, for the man and his wife delighted to know and to do the will of God. They welcomed the presence and the voice of God. Communion with Him was the reason for their existence.

Perhaps you have experienced something of that kind of relationship with God. You have been the recipient of His incredible love and blessing; you know what it is to walk with Him, to listen to His Word, and to respond with the worship of a satisfied heart.

Do you also know what it is to lose that intimacy? Do you know what it is to make a choice that creates distance where there was once nearness, fear where there was once trust, and shame where there was once freedom?

That moment when the first man and first woman signed their own emancipation proclamation was a decisive one. They chose to believe the word of the serpent rather than the word of God. They acted apart from God and became separated from God. Now when they heard the sound of God walking in the garden in the early morning hours, they were fearful and could not bear to face Him or each other. Instead, they covered their naked bodies and attempted to hide from God.

As the daughters of Eve, we have all experienced that fearful, dreadful sense of shame that makes us want to hide from God because we know we have spurned the only true love we have ever known. In that dark instant, we may feel that we have thrown His love away and will never experience it again.

But even in that moment of shameful separation in the garden, there was hope, as God the Eternal Lover took the initiative to restore the estranged couple to fellowship. By means of a sacrifice, He tenderly, lovingly clothed them in the skins of animals and set in motion the events whereby man might ultimately be reunited with Him. And all the time, God never stopped loving, never stopped communicating, never stopped seeking, never stopped initiating. Just as He never stops loving and seeking you and me.

Abraham: Friend of God

Centuries later, in keeping with His great, eternal plan, God revealed Himself to another man. I have often tried to imagine what Abraham must have felt the very first time he heard the voice of God. Abraham was not looking for God—he did not even know there was a God. He had been reared in a pagan, idolatrous culture where not one single person had ever known God. There were no believers, no Bibles, no hymnals, no churches, no Sunday school classes, no preachers—only deafening silence from heaven.

Then one day, God pierced the silence. He introduced Himself to Abraham and made some incredible promises. Abraham heard the voice of God. And Abraham believed God.

When no one else was listening, when no one else believed, Abraham was given grace to respond to God's initiative. The story of Abraham's life is the story of a man who listened to the voice of God as He revealed His secrets, His plans, and His will. It is the story of a man who responded to the voice of his Beloved in worship, faith, love, and obedience. Altars erected at Shechem, Bethel, Hebron, and Mount Moriah trace the steps of this "friend of God"—a man who walked with God in intimate communion and fellowship.

It's not that Abraham never wavered in his faith. In fact, on more than one occasion, he acted as if he didn't know God at all. But God's love was not based on Abraham's performance. Even when Abraham started acting like a pagan, God pursued him passionately and relentlessly. Just as He did Adam and Eve. Just as He does you and me.

David: "One Thing Have I Desired"

Fourteen generations after Abraham, another friend of God continued a line that would lead to the Lord Jesus Himself. As a military strategist and warrior, as a musician and poet, and as a statesman and king—in virtually every way—David stood head and shoulders above the men of his day.

This man had it all—fame, popularity, fortune, natural ability, and loyal friends. So when David says, "One thing have I desired of the LORD, that will I seek after" (Psalm 27:4 KJV), we wonder, What is the deepest desire and longing of this man's heart? What matters to him more than anything else? What is his highest earthly priority? If only one thing could be said of him at the end of his life, what would he want it to be?

By the way, how would *you* finish that sentence? "One thing have I desired of the Lord; that will I seek after: _____." What is the greatest desire and longing of your heart? In the answer to that question lies the explanation for much of what we do—our choices, our priorities, our use of time, the way we spend money, the way we respond to pressure, whom or what we love. David's answer reveals why God could say, "This man's heart beats like Mine":

> One thing have I desired of the LORD, that will I seek after; that I may dwell in the house of the LORD all the days of my life, to behold the beauty of the LORD, and to enquire in his temple. (PSALM 27:4 KJV)

In spite of all he possessed, all he had done, all the people he had known, all the places he had been, and all the privileges and opportunities he had enjoyed, David had one supreme, driving passion in life: to walk in intimate union and communion with God. It is as if he were saying, "If I can only accomplish one thing in my life, if nothing else gets done, this is the one thing that really matters to me; this is my highest goal and my number one priority: to *live* in the presence of the Lord, to *look* on His beauty, and to *learn* from Him. I want to know Him, to love Him, to have an intimate relationship with Him. That's the one thing in my life that matters most. And that is the one thing I am going to pursue above all others."

Like Abraham, David had his flaws. He blew it in some of the most crucial relationships of life. But this Lover-God would not let him go. With a confronting, convicting, consuming, cleansing love, God pursued His beloved. At points, one might have wondered, Why does God bother with *him*? The answer is the same reason He bothers with us—because He is a Lover in pursuit of relationship—a God who never stops loving and pursuing.

Mary and Martha of Bethany: "Only One Thing Is Needed"

The New Testament introduces us to another familiar figure, this time a woman who enjoyed an intimate love relationship with her Lord and who treasured time spent alone in His presence. Actually, the story of Mary of Bethany is closely intertwined with that of her sister, Martha. It is a story that speaks to me afresh each time I read it.

We first meet the two women in Luke 10:38–42, where we are told that "Martha opened her home to [Jesus]" (v. 38). What a wonderful thing to be said of a woman! Martha was the "hostess with the mostest"—the sister with an extraordinary flair for hospitality.

How we need women today who are willing to open their hearts and homes to others. In a day when the majority of women are devoting their best hours to jobs outside their homes, there are so few who have a heart for hospitality—for serving and ministering to others, whether in their home, at church, in a restaurant, or in a park.

As the passage unfolds, we see a dramatic scene that I recognize all too well. A band of hungry men descends on Martha's home. I can just imagine this highly organized, efficient woman as she flies into action. She is giving orders to everyone within earshot—there is no time to waste; this is no time to dawdle; the bread must be kneaded and baked; the meat must be prepared and grilled; the vegetables must be scrubbed and boiled; the floors must be cleaned, tables set, drinks poured . . .

As you read the passage, you can sense that things aren't falling together quite right, and you watch as this capable woman begins to get edgy and agitated; there is just no way everything will be ready on time! We are told, "Martha was distracted by all the preparations that had to be made" (v. 40). The King James Version puts it this way: "Martha was cumbered about much serving." That word *cumbered* literally means "to be pulled apart."[1] Do you know that feeling? I certainly do.

We start out with the best intentions to serve those around us. But one circumstance piles on top of another until we become so consumed with the mechanics and details of our work that we begin to feel pulled apart and lose sight of why we were serving in the first place.

I've had it happen in the kitchen, in the midst of preparing dessert for a Bible study group. I've had it happen in my study, while preparing messages for a women's conference. I've had it happen in the church, while pulling together details for a Sunday school class.

Perhaps it was when she forgot to set the timer and the rolls burned that Martha's simmering frustration finally began to boil as she looked around and realized that her younger sister was nowhere to be seen. "Where's Mary?!" she demanded of the nearest servant. "She's in the living room with the men." That did it. Martha had had it!

When the explosion came, it was directed not at Mary but

at Jesus. "Lord," she remonstrated, "don't you care that my sister has left me to do the work by myself?" (v. 40). When we become preoccupied with earthly things rather than eternal matters, we become resentful, self-centered, and angry. Our party turns into a pity party, and we start to believe that no one—not even Jesus—knows or cares about all the sacrifices we've made. "Tell her to help me!" she demanded. (Have you ever found yourself telling *God* what to do?)

The reason most of us relate to the story thus far is because we know what it is to have our inner spirit in turmoil; to become irritated, angry, and demanding; to feel as if our circumstances and our emotions have spun out of control. After the explosion, we feel terrible and we think, "What got into me? Why did I act that way? Why did I get so uptight and frustrated over something as insignificant as burned rolls?"

Jesus' words to Martha speak to the Martha in all of us. Patiently He addressed her: "Martha, Martha, . . . you are worried and upset about many things, but *only one thing is needed*. Mary has chosen what is better, and it will not be taken away from her" (Luke 10:41–42, emphasis added).

What is it that Mary had chosen? What was Mary doing all this time? She was simply sitting at the feet of Jesus "listening to what he said" (v. 39).

It is as if Jesus were saying, "Martha, there are so many things on your mind, so many items on your 'to do' list. There's nothing wrong with your wanting to serve us dinner. The problem is that you have allowed your 'to do' list to pull you apart and to distract you from the only thing in this world that really matters—knowing Me, listening to Me, having a relationship with Me. That is the only thing that is absolutely essential. If you don't get anything else done on your list, don't miss that one thing!"

Jesus reminded Martha that Mary had made a *choice* to cultivate her relationship with the Master. Developing intimacy with the Lord Jesus requires a conscious, deliberate choice. It is a choice to spend time sitting at His feet and listening to His

Word, even when there are other good things that are demanding our attention. It is a choice to put Him first, above all our other responsibilities and tasks.

I can almost hear Jesus saying to Martha, "We don't have to have a five-course meal tonight. It's OK with Me if we just have soup and crackers. It's OK if dinner's late, if the rolls get burned, or even if we don't have dinner at all. None of that really matters. What matters is My relationship with you. That's why I came to your house. That's why I came to this world. Your company means more to Me than your cooking. *You* are more important to Me than anything you can *do* for Me."

And so we're right back where we started, realizing that God is a Lover who created us for relationship with Himself. That's what the Christian life is all about. It is not about all the things we do for God—it's about being loved by Him, loving Him in return, and walking in intimate union and communion with Him.

Mary's choice was not made out of obligation, but out of devotion. She was not sitting at His feet out of a sense of duty, but because she cherished her relationship with the Lord Jesus.

Shortly before He went to the cross, Mary attended another dinner where Jesus was a guest, this time at the home of Simon the leper (John 12:1–8). Once again, we find Martha serving (though I'd like to think she served this meal with a different heart!). And once again, we find Mary at the feet of Jesus, this time anointing His feet with a pound of costly ointment. The act, though it incurred the indignation of some who watched, was precious to Jesus, for He knew His love had won her heart.

"*Devotions*" Without "Devotion"

Some of us have had *devotions*, but we've not had *devotion*. There's a big difference. We may have gone through the motions of reading our Bibles and "saying our prayers," but we have not been cultivating a love relationship with our Lover-God.

We know a lot *about* Him, but we don't really know *Him*. We are active and busy in a multitude of spiritual activities, but we have lost perspective of who it is that we are serving and why.

The result of our "devotionless" religion is seen in the way we respond to pressure. So many of us as Christian women are chronically stressed out. Everywhere I go, I see it in the eyes of women; I hear it in their voices; and too often I see it when I look in my own mirror. I know what it is to have demands coming at me from every direction. I know what it is to respond out of weariness, with an impatient, demanding spirit. And I know what it is to contend with God Himself, even as my eyes fill up with tears of frustration with myself and my reactions.

I also know that there is only one place where that angry, reactive, overwhelmed self can be transformed—the same place that Mary chose—the feet of Jesus. I must make a conscious, deliberate, daily choice to sit at His feet, to listen to His Word, to receive His love, to let Him change me, and to pour out my heart's devotion to Him.

When I get into His presence, the whole world looks different. When I draw close to His heart, I find mercy when I know I deserve judgment; I find forgiveness for all my petty, selfish ways; I find grace for all my inadequacies; I find peace for my troubled heart; I find perspective for my distorted views. In Him, I find an eye in the midst of the storm. Oh, the storm around me may not immediately subside; but the storm *within* me is made calm.

An Invitation to Intimacy

And so the Father-Lover heart of God continues to call us into relationship with Himself. He is seeking lovers. He is always thinking about us, always desiring our company and our fellowship; He longs to hear our voice and see our face.

Not until we make pursuing Him our highest priority and goal in life will we begin to fulfill the purpose for which He created us. Nothing—absolutely nothing—is more important. And that relationship for which we were created cannot be cultivated or sustained apart from spending consistent time alone with Him.

Where are you in your relationship with Him? Is it intimate, vital, and growing? Or has it become distant and passionless? Are you nurturing that relationship by spending time each day alone with Him? Is He giving you a new desire to know Him and His love and to offer true devotion to Him? If so, why not take David's mission statement (Psalm 27:4) and make it your prayer:

Lord Jesus, You have shown me that only one thing is absolutely necessary, and that is the one thing I want to seek after with all my heart: that I may live in Your presence every day of my life, that I may gaze upon Your beauty with a heart of worship and adoration, and that I may learn to know Your heart, Your ways, and Your will. To this supreme purpose I dedicate myself. By Your grace, I will make this the highest daily priority of my life. Amen.

MAKING IT PERSONAL

1. Whom do you know who seems to have an intimate, personal relationship with the Lord? To what do you attribute his or her closeness to God?

2. Martha was "pulled apart" by all her meal preparations. What are some of the things that pull you apart and keep you from sitting at the feet of Jesus and listening to Him?

3. If someone were to look at the way you spend your time, what would he or she say are the most important priorities in your life?

4. Describe a time in your life when taking time out to "sit at the feet of Jesus" made a noticeable difference in your perspective or your ability to respond to your circumstances.

FROM THE HEART OF

Nancy Wilson

As in any relationship, it is absolutely essential to keep my heart in touch with the Lord's. How can a relationship flourish without sharing intimate time together? The consistency of that time cultivates the practice of His presence in my daily life and ministry. I tell Him that He is the number one priority in my life and give Him the opportunity to redirect my steps according to His assignments and purposes for me. My chief desire is to keep my first love burning brightly.

Sometimes the busyness of a travel schedule makes it difficult to carve out adequate time. But I have purposed in my heart that He will be first and have found ways to choose Him above other things. For example, if I'm at a conference, I will often skip breakfast to spend that time with the Lord. Or I will arrange a special time in my schedule to pull away and meet with Him.

When I'm not feeling good about myself, I find I'm not as eager to run to my Abba Father. I've been learning to stand against wrong thinking, to resist the Enemy, and to run into the arms of my loving Father through focusing on His truth, His promises, and His incredible love and desire for me. I often think about being His beloved Bride and how cherished I am by Him. That gives me a greater desire to meet with Him and helps me see His refining process as a preparation for spending eternity with Him.

I have come to treasure the place of the Word in my life. I use it in prayer, in praise, in confronting the lies of the Enemy, and in seeking God's voice.

Worshiping God turns my attention to His worth-ship. Praise takes my eyes off myself and places them upon the worthy One. Though I see my own unworthiness, I'm also freshly aware of His incredible grace. I must press on into the Holy Place by the blood of Jesus. Then I can come boldly to the throne of grace to find mercy and grace to help in time of need. What a precious Savior, Bridegroom, and King!

Nancy Wilson is the associate national director of Student Venture, the high school outreach of Campus Crusade for Christ. A single woman, Nancy is actively involved in sharing the gospel of Jesus Christ with young people and women across the United States and around the world.

NOTE

1. *The Wycliffe Bible Commentary*, ed. Everett F. Harrison (Chicago: Moody, 1990), 1047.

PART TWO

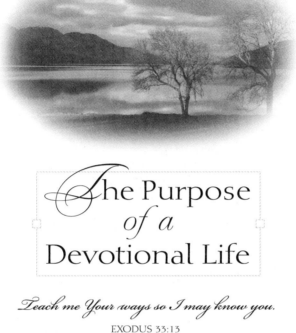

The Purpose
of a
Devotional Life

Teach me Your ways so I may know you.

EXODUS 33:13

The young believer must understand that he has no power of his own to maintain his spiritual life. No, he needs each day to receive new grace from heaven through fellowship with the Lord Jesus. This cannot be obtained by a hasty prayer, or a superficial reading of a few verses from God's Word. He must take time quietly and deliberately to come into God's presence, to feel his weakness and his need, and to wait upon God through His Holy Spirit to renew the heavenly light and life in his heart. Then he may rightly expect to be kept by the power of Christ throughout all the day and all its temptations.

ANDREW MURRAY

CHAPTER 3

The Inner Life

Deep down, have you ever had any of these thoughts?

If I have my devotions, God will be pleased with me. If I don't have my devotions, God will be disappointed with me.

Having daily devotions makes me more spiritual. If I don't have daily devotions, I am less spiritual.

If I have devotions today, God will help me out and my day will go better. If I don't have devotions, God won't help me, and I'm sure to have all sorts of problems.

I have to have daily devotions—every good Christian does.

We have looked at the *priority* of spending time alone with God on a consistent basis. We have seen that Jesus felt it was imperative that He establish and maintain regular times of communication with His Father. We have observed that a distinguishing characteristic of godly men and women in the Scripture was that the one thing that mattered most to them was knowing God. We have said that spending time with God must be the number one priority of our lives if we are to fulfill the purpose for which God created us.

Now we turn to look more specifically at the *purpose* of spending time alone with God. One of the major reasons people experience a sense of frustration and failure in their devotional life is because they don't understand *why* such a habit is important. As a result, there are sincere believers who have (or try to have) daily devotions for all the wrong reasons.

Thoughts such as those listed above have put many believers in bondage and kept them from entering into the real purpose for setting aside time each day to meet with God.

We need to understand that having daily devotions is *not* for the purpose of getting extra points with God—nor is it a way to keep God from disapproving of us; we are not trying to earn His favor or get Him to love us more. If we belong to Him, we already *have* His favor; He could not love us any more and He could not love us any less.

Further, setting aside time for devotional activity, in and of itself, does not necessarily make us any more spiritual. (The Pharisees were renowned for their "devotional habits," but they were far from spiritual.) Neither is a quiet time some sort of good luck charm that gets God on our side, guarantees our day will go better, and keeps us from having problems. Daily devotions are not a way of bartering or negotiating with God.

Then what *is* the purpose of devotions? What makes it worth making the effort to get up earlier in the morning, to find time in an already hectic schedule, and to prioritize a daily quiet time? What are we hoping to see accomplished through that time? And why is this habit such a crucial one in the life of a believer? I'd like to suggest eight purposes I have discovered. The first four relate primarily to our inner life with God, and we will discuss them in this chapter. In the next chapter we will consider four additional purposes that affect not only our inner life but flow out into our lifestyle and our relationships with others.

Communion

The most important purpose of a daily devotional life is not so that we can check another task off our "to do" list, but rather, that we might experience intimate union and communion with God. Remember, we are talking about a relationship. The God of the universe *loves you*, and He created you to be His *friend*. You say, "Is that really possible? How can someone like me have a close friendship with God?" Moses must have wondered the same thing at one time.

Moses and God came to experience an extraordinary relationship. But it didn't start out that way. In fact, Moses' first encounter with God could hardly be called intimate. As he stood next to that piece of burning brush on the side of a mountain and heard the voice of God, Moses was terrified. The Scripture says that he "hid his face, because he was afraid to look at God" (Exodus 3:6).

But once God had Moses' attention, He began to share with Moses things no other man of his time had ever known. He revealed His compassionate heart and His deep concern about the sufferings of the children of Israel in Egypt. He revealed His desire to deliver His people from slavery. He revealed His plan to use Moses as His instrument. And He revealed that He had all the power and resources to make it happen.

As Moses thought back over his checkered past and his very average aptitudes, he must have wondered how this could be. He felt insecure, overwhelmed, and inadequate (ever had those feelings yourself?). Nonetheless, he responded to God's initiative, and from that day his life was never the same—just as your life will never be the same once you embark on the adventure of a growing, vital relationship with God.

For the most part, over the next forty years Moses communed alone with God, for, with the exception of Joshua, there were few others who had the same heart to know God. Perhaps you know what it is to walk alone with God, without the fellowship of a godly mate, children, or close friends. Be encouraged that, though there may be no one near you who is committed to walk with God, you can still enjoy personal communion with God.

After leading the children of Israel out of Egypt and across the Red Sea, Moses continued to devote himself to pursuing communion with God. At times, that meant responding to God's call to spend extended days alone with Him in remote mountain settings.

During one of those protracted times, God gave His servant directions for constructing a tabernacle. God described the purpose of this tent-structure: "There I will meet you and speak to you; there also I will meet with the Israelites" (Exodus 29:42–43). The purpose of the tabernacle (and later of the temple) was that there might be a place on this earth where God could commune with His people. For centuries, if an Israelite wanted to meet with God, to fellowship with Him, he would go to the meeting place God had established for that purpose.

When we come to the New Testament, we learn that we no longer need to go to a physical tent or place of meeting to commune with God. Because Christ has come and shed His blood for our sins, the way has been opened up for us to approach the Father directly, without the need for a human mediator. By His indwelling Holy Spirit, you and I have become the temple of God, the very place where God dwells.

The purpose of this new temple is the same as it was with the temple of old—a place where we can come and commune with God. This is the heart of Jesus' words to the church in Laodicea: "Here I am! I stand at the door and knock. If anyone hears my voice and opens the door, I will come in and eat with him, and he with me" (Revelation 3:20). Eating a meal together is a universal symbol of friendship and fellowship. As with Moses, the purpose of our devotional time is not to jump through spiritual hoops or to fulfill some sort of heavenly homework assignment, but to sit down and eat a fellowship meal with the Lord—to commune with Him.

As a result of extended time spent in the presence of God, Moses enjoyed an unusually deep friendship with God. Whereas others in the camp could not draw near to God or look on His glory, "the LORD would speak to Moses face to face, as a man speaks with his friend" (Exodus 33:11). Moses was not allowed to see God's face (vv. 21–33), but God spoke with Moses directly, not through an intermediary.

FACE-TO-FACE FRIENDSHIP

"Face to face" in Exodus 33:11 is a picture of intimacy. It is a picture of lovers. On the other hand, when something comes between two friends, it can be awkward and uncomfortable to be face-to-face. I remember hearing a wife describe a disagreement she had had with her husband the night before. She said, "I lay down on our bed and turned my face toward the wall and my back toward my husband!" It doesn't take a therapist to know there's a problem in that relationship. The intimacy has been breached.

You have seen the same principle at work in children. When your child does something wrong, where is the last place in the world he wants to look? In your eyes. Holding his little face in your hands, you say sternly, "Look in Mommy's eyes!" But he avoids looking in your face. Why? Because something has come between the two of you, and the fellowship has been broken.

If you have walked with God for any length of time, you know what it is to have a breach in the relationship—to find it difficult to look Him "in the eyes." The purpose of a daily devotional time is to get back into His presence, to find out what has caused the breach, and to reestablish fellowship. Then we can once again look in His face without shame or fear.

We see in Moses a man who was always yearning for a deeper, more intimate fellowship with God. In one of his most intimate recorded conversations with God, Moses pled, "If you are pleased with me, teach me your ways so I may know you" (Exodus 33:13). This is the prayer of a man who didn't just want to know more *about* God. He wanted to *know* God.

As you meet with God in your daily devotional time, don't forget that the ultimate purpose is not simply to gain more knowledge about God or His Word, but to know *Him* and to enjoy intimate communion with Him. You may be a seasoned student of the Word. You may even be a Bible study leader. But if your study of the Word does not lead you to *know God*, you have missed the whole purpose.

In the front of my Bible, I have written these words that express my longing to come to know God through His Word:

> Beyond the sacred page,
> I seek *Thee*, Lord.
> My spirit pants for *Thee*,
> O living Word.

—MARY A. LATHBURY (1841–1913), emphasis added

 urification

Do you sometimes feel like all you ever do is clean? That's because things (and people) tend to get dirty. Whether clothes, children's hands, kitchen floors, bathrooms, vinyl siding, entryways, or our bodies—dealing with the dust, crumbs, and grime that accumulate is a necessary and never-ending process.

The second purpose of a devotional life is purification, or cleansing of our hearts and our lives. Now, as far as our *position* before God is concerned, we have already been declared righteous, for the Lord Jesus has taken all our unrighteousness upon Himself and clothed us in His righteousness.

As far as our future *prospect* is concerned, "before the foundation of the world," God chose us and determined "that we should be holy and without blame before him" (Ephesians 1:4 KJV). He predestined us to be a holy bride for His holy Son—and one day we will be just that.

However, as far as our *practice* is concerned, we do not always live up to our holy position and our holy prospect. You and I live in a corrupt world. We inhabit a contaminated flesh. And we have a way of getting our spiritual feet, hands, and clothes soiled.

At the Last Supper, taking the place of a slave, Jesus went around the table, washing the feet of each of the disciples. When He came to Peter, He taught an important lesson about this matter of cleansing. Peter was not comfortable with the whole idea of the Master's washing his feet. In response to Peter's protest, Jesus told him that apart from being washed he could have no part with Christ.

The pure, spotless, undefiled Son of God cannot walk in oneness with impure, defiled believers. "Can two walk together, except they be agreed?" the prophet asked (Amos 3:3 KJV). "Your iniquities have separated you from your God," Isaiah explained to worshipers who wanted to know why God wasn't listening to their prayers (Isaiah 59:2).

When Peter realized the cost of refusing cleansing, he decided he wanted to go all the way. "'Then, Lord,' Simon Peter replied, 'not just my feet but my hands and my head as well!'" (John 13:9).

Jesus went on to explain that "a person who has had a bath needs only to wash his feet; his whole body is clean. And you are clean" (v. 10). In other words, once we enter into a relationship with Christ through His shed blood, we have been eternally cleansed. But when we allow our lives to become soiled by this world or by our own natural choices, we need to return to be washed once more.

In the Old Testament tabernacle, we find a striking picture of this process of washing. Before entering into the Holy Place to represent the people before God, the priest would first stop at the bronze altar where an innocent animal would be offered up as a sacrifice for his own sin and for the sin of the people. Then the priest would move to a bronze basin known as a laver, where he would wash his hands. He would return to that laver as needed throughout the day. Although our sin has been atoned for by the blood of Jesus, when we come into His presence, He takes us to the laver that we might wash our hands and feet of whatever may have defiled us.

WASHED WITH THE WATER OF THE WORD

What is the "water" God uses to purify us? It is the water of the Word. Jesus prayed for His disciples, "Sanctify them by the truth; your word is truth" (John 17:17). In His final discourse with the disciples before going to Gethsemane, Jesus said, "Now ye are clean through the word which I have spoken unto you" (John 15:3 KJV).

The book of Ephesians teaches that "Christ loved the church and gave himself up for her" (Ephesians 5:25). His death on the cross was birthed out of His commitment to a love relationship. The next verse goes on to reveal His ultimate purpose for the church and how He intends to fulfill that purpose: "to make her holy, cleansing her by the washing with water *through the word*" (v. 5:26, emphasis added). The Holy Spirit takes the Word and applies it to our hearts to cleanse and purify them. Frequently, both before and after reading the Word, I will ask God to use the Word to wash the innermost parts of my heart.

As I spend time alone with God in the morning, I ask Him who sees and knows all to expose anything in my heart that is not holy. He knows me better than I know myself. My natural tendency would be to cover my sin, so I ask Him to shine the light of His holiness into my heart and to show me what He sees there. Through worship, prayer, and the Word, I step out of the darkness into His light and pray,

> *Who can understand his errors? cleanse thou me from secret faults. . . . Search me, O God, and know my heart: try me, and know my thoughts: and see if there be any wicked way in me, and lead me in the way everlasting.* (PSALMS 19:12; 139:23–24 KJV)

Day after day, as I open up my heart to His light, He is faithful to bring to my attention that which has grieved Him—a harsh word spoken to an employee, a selfish choice or expenditure, a haughty or unloving attitude toward another, a covetous heart, unbelief, an impatient response, seeking human praise or admiration, taking credit for what He has done, an ungrateful spirit, unforgiveness or resentment, demanding rights . . .

Having seen what the light reveals, I agree with God, confess it as sin, and ask Him to cleanse me by the blood and the Word of Christ. Where my sin has affected others, I purpose to seek their forgiveness. Then I am free to walk before Him, without guilt or shame, and with a pure heart and a conscience that is clear toward God and all men.

Having cleansed us from sin by the washing of His Word, God then uses the Scripture to protect our hearts from sinning against Him. "How can a young man keep his way pure? By living according to your word" (Psalm 119:9).

Restoration

Ask any woman today how she's doing, and there's a good chance the answer will be "Busy!" or "Exhausted!" Overcrowded schedules and stressed-out lives seem to be the order of the day. I don't think the issue is just a matter of how much we have to do. If it were, all we'd need is a vacation. But you've probably had the experience, as I have, of taking time off, only to come back more exhausted than when you left. I'm convinced that one of the major reasons we can't handle the demands of day-to-day living is that our *spirits* are weary. Our *souls* need to be restored. And that is another purpose of setting aside time to be alone in God's presence each day.

As we walk through each day, responding to the needs of those around us, we can become physically, emotionally, and spiritually depleted. God has a never-ending supply of grace, strength, and wisdom available that He wants to flow through us to others. And we need to keep coming back into His presence to get our supply replenished.

The circumstances and demands of a typical day may cause us to fall wearily into bed at night. But when we awake in the morning, His mercies are new and fresh (Lamentations 3:23). If we fail to stop and draw from His fresh, infinite supply of mercy and grace, we will find ourselves having to operate out of our own depleted, meager resources.

The psalmist knew what it was to get his soul restored in the presence of God. Many of the psalms begin with expressions of fear, terror, anger, frustration, or confusion. But as he pours out his heart to the Lord, his whole perspective is changed, and he receives a fresh infusion of supernatural hope and strength.

Listen to the prayer of David when he is out in the wilderness fleeing from an insanely jealous king who is obsessed with taking his life:

> *O God, you are my God,*
>   *earnestly I seek you;*
> *my soul thirsts for you,*
>   *my body longs for you,*
> *in a dry and weary land*
>   *where there is no water. . . .*
>
> *Because your love is better than life,*
>   *my lips will glorify you. . . .*
> *My soul will be satisfied as with the richest of foods. . . .*
>
> *Because you are my help,*
>   *I sing in the shadow of your wings.*
>
> —PSALM 63:1, 3, 5, 7

You can sense the restoration taking place in David's soul as he cries out to God in the midst of another crisis:
Hear my cry, O God;

listen to my prayer.
From the ends of the earth I call to you,
  I call as my heart grows faint;
  lead me to the rock that is higher than I.
For you have been my refuge,
  a strong tower against the foe.

I long to dwell in your tent forever
  and take refuge in the shelter of your wings.
  —PSALM 61:1–4

The restoration of our souls is a ministry of our Great Shepherd. "The Lord is my shepherd, I shall not be in want. . . . He restores my soul" (Psalm 23:1, 3). The Hebrew word translated "restore" in Psalm 23 is a word that is more often translated "return" in the Old Testament. It is used to speak of God's people returning to Him and of God returning to His people. The word suggests "movement back to the point of departure."[1] The implication here is that He restores our souls back to their original resting place—in Him. He does so by means of His Spirit and His Word: "He makes me lie down in green pastures, he leads me beside quiet waters" (Psalm 23:2). Notice that the sheep don't get fed, refreshed, and restored on the run. They must be willing to slow down, to stop at times, to be still, to lie down.

Often I find myself giving out and giving out and giving out, but not taking time to get back to the still, quiet waters where my Shepherd wants to restore my soul. If I don't take time to get my spiritual tank refilled, I soon find myself "running on fumes." Before long, the least little demand is more than I can handle, and I find myself reacting to even minor annoyances and interruptions out of frustration and irritation.

It is in those daily devotional times alone with Him that He calms my spirit, slows down my racing pulse, and gives me fresh perspective and renewed desire and strength to serve Him another day.

Even as you read these words, is your soul in need of

restoration? Why not take a few minutes to reread the two prayers of David quoted above. Try reading them aloud. As you do, let your Great Shepherd restore your soul.

Instruction

Wouldn't it be great if there were a class you could take that would teach you everything you needed to know and provide answers for all your problems? Maybe you've got a boss who is impossible to please, a food addiction you just can't kick, a husband who watches TV all the time, a church where no one seems to be hungry for God, a child who has started lying, or bills that always seem larger than the paycheck.

The fact is, there *is* a "course" that addresses every issue we will ever face. The Teacher loves to meet one-on-one with His students, so that He can tailor the course to our needs. He is willing to hold class every day that we are willing to meet. We already have the Textbook, which was written by the Teacher Himself. Parts of it can be difficult to grasp. But the Teacher is always available—twenty-four hours a day—to help us understand.

Establishing a daily devotional habit enrolls us in this course. During this time, we can sit at the feet of the Lord Jesus and ask Him to instruct us, to teach us what He is like and how to live in a way that pleases Him.

The Textbook—the Word of God—doesn't claim to solve all our problems. (The fact is, God isn't as interested in solving our *problems* as He is in changing *us*.) But it does claim to have all the resources we need to face those problems. And it will teach us something that is absolutely essential to dealing with the circumstances of life: *the ways of God*.

Psalm 103:7 (KJV) tells us that God "made known his *ways* unto Moses, his *acts* unto the children of Israel" (emphasis added). There is a big difference between knowing the acts of God and knowing His ways. All the Israelites saw the *acts* of God—they saw Him send the plagues on the Egyptians when

Pharaoh hardened his heart against God; they saw Him part the waters of the Red Sea when there was no other way of escape from the Egyptian army; when they were hungry, they saw God provide manna for bread and quail for meat; when they were thirsty, they saw Him bring water gushing forth from a rock; when Miriam challenged Moses' right to lead, they saw God strike her with leprosy—they were well-acquainted with the *acts* of God.

But they knew little of the *ways* of God. God revealed His ways to Moses because Moses had an attentive heart, a listening ear, and a passion to know God. Moses was willing to pay the price to know God's ways. He was willing to spend much time alone with God, away from the crowd, patiently waiting for God to speak.

"SHOW ME YOUR WAYS"

One of the greatest desires of my heart and one of my most frequent prayers is that I might know the ways of God. I want to know His thoughts, His feelings, His heart, and even His secrets. I want to know His perspective on this world, on history, on current affairs, on the future, on work, relaxation, relationships, my family, the church, and ministry—on everything. I want to know what brings Him joy and what causes Him to grieve. I want to know His ways. I don't believe God owes me an explanation about anything. But I do want to know everything about Him and His heart that He is willing to reveal.

That is why virtually every day, before I open the Word of God, I pray the words of David in Psalm 25:4–5:

> *Show me your ways, O LORD,*
> *teach me your paths;*
> *guide me in your truth and teach me.*

That psalm goes on to tell us the kind of man or woman that God will teach:

He guides the humble *in what is right
and teaches them his way. . . .*

Who, then, is the man that fears *the* LORD?
He will instruct him in the way chosen for him. . . .
The LORD *confides in those* who *fear him;
he makes his covenant known to them.*

—PSALM 25:9, 12, 14, emphasis added

Whom does the Lord teach? He instructs those whose hearts are humble ("meek," KJV)— those who have a teachable spirit, those who know how little they know and how much they need to learn. And He teaches those who fear Him— those who reverence and stand in awe of Him. Those are the ones He "confides in." The King James Version translates verse 14: "The secret of the LORD is with them that fear him; and he will shew them his covenant." What an awesome thought— that the God of the universe would confide in us, that He would trust us with His secrets. God's willingness to share the secrets of His heart with His creatures is just another evidence of His desire to have an intimate relationship and friendship with us.

I have been an avid reader and student since I was a little girl. I always loved school and made good grades. There are some topics on which I have read a great deal over the years. But when I come into God's presence and hold His Word in my hand, I feel so very ignorant, insignificant, and needy of His instruction. Further, I feel an incredible sense of awe that He would stoop to reveal the secrets of His heart to me. Surely such riches are worth whatever time, discipline, and sacrifice are necessary to mine them from His treasure-store.

My undergraduate degree is in piano performance. From time to time, the university I attended would offer "master classes" in which master teachers would teach the secrets they had acquired over many years of study and performance. But nothing can compare to the joy and privilege of sitting and learning at the feet of our heavenly Master, "in whom are hidden all the treasures of wisdom and knowledge" (Colossians 2:3).

MAKING IT PERSONAL

1. What are some inferior motivations you have sometimes had for having a quiet time?

2. Think of someone with whom you share a particularly close relationship. What are some of the elements that have contributed to developing and maintaining that friendship?

   How might those elements apply to cultivating an intimate relationship with the Lord?

3. Record an instance in which God used His Word to cleanse your heart, to restore your soul, or to teach you something of His ways.

4. Write a brief paragraph expressing why you want to cultivate a consistent devotional life. Focus on your need for more intimate communion with Him, for purification, for restoration of your soul, or for instruction.

5. Read aloud the prayer of David in Psalm 25:4–5. Then pray it back to God in your own words.

FROM THE HEART OF
Sandy Smith

The purpose of a daily quiet time is to know God. As we know Him more intimately, obedience will become a matter of love rather than fear; service to others will be an outpouring of His love rather than duty; trust will become a natural response to His character; and our lives will bring glory to Him.

Drawing apart to begin the day by communing with our Father shifts our focus and fixes our hearts. We begin to see God in every circumstance and receive interruptions as from Him. Without this time, our days become harried and frustrating and we often miss great opportunities He sends our way.

A quiet spirit results from a consistent time alone with God because we have surrendered ourselves to His sovereign plan for that day. We gain a settled confidence that God is in complete control of every circumstance of our lives.

I have found that it takes a firm commitment to make daily devotions consistent. However, I have often felt guilty if this time isn't as long as I think it should be or if I don't cover all the disciplines I think are important. It has taken years for me to realize that God doesn't love me because I have a quiet time—He just loves me! This knowledge alone has increased my desire to be with Him.

How important it is to come to our quiet time, not with the fear that God will punish us if we miss, but eager to meet Him—to learn, to grow, and to find sweet fellowship with a Father who loves us far more than we could ever imagine.

Sandy Smith is the wife of evangelist Bailey Smith and the mother of three grown sons. Each year Sandy and her husband host several national conferences for the purpose of nurturing and equipping women in their walk with God.

NOTES

PART PAGE: Andrew Murray, *The Secret of Fellowship* (Fort Washington, Pa.: Christian Literature Crusade, 1981), Introduction.

1. *The Complete Word Study Old Testament* (Chattanooga: AMG, 1994), 2372.

CHAPTER 4

The
Outer Walk

Are you thirsty for a more intimate relationship with God? Do you want a heart that is pure and free from sin? Do you want Him to restore your soul each day? Do you want Him to teach you His ways? We have discovered that these are four key reasons for spending time alone with God on a daily basis. But that's not all. There is more that the Lord wants to do in our lives as we sit at His feet and linger in His presence.

We turn now to four other significant purposes. As the Holy Spirit fulfills each of these objectives in our hearts, the result will be seen in the way we live our lives toward God and others.

Submission

As we spend time alone with God, our lives are brought into submission to God and His will. I will be the first to admit that the "S" word is not one of the most popular words in our free-spirited era. Neither does submission come naturally. I don't think I've met anybody yet who was "born submissive." I surely wasn't. I came into this world with a strong, independent will that wanted to be in control of everybody and everything around me. So did you. The idea of submitting to the control or will of another is utterly contrary to our old nature.

When we became children of God, we received a new nature, a nature that recognizes God's right to rule over us and wants to please Him and submit to His will. However, although our spirit wants to obey God, our "flesh" (that is, our natural inclination) wars against our spirit and wants to have its own way.

As a result, there are times when we resent, resist, or run from the circumstances God has brought into our lives. When an annoying or difficult circumstance arises, we tend to view the troublesome person or circumstance as our problem and to resist the pressure it places upon us. In so doing, we end up pushing against God Himself and resisting His will for our lives. We may do so overtly, or there may just be a "kick" in our spirit.

The problem is that we have failed to see the hand of God in bringing this situation into our lives. He is wanting to use it to train us, to mold us into the image of His Son, and to develop godly character in us.

Left to ourselves, we will continue to chafe under the circumstance until finally we are destroyed by bitterness and resentment.

But when we take time to enter into God's presence and wait quietly before Him, when we place our lives under the ministry and microscope of His Word, our resistance is exposed, we see the sovereign hand of God that is acting for our own good, and we realize the folly of trying to "box" with God.

As His Spirit works within us, our spirits are once again made pliable and brought into submission to God's authority, and we are able to joyously embrace His will. An evidence that our will has been broken is that we begin to thank God for that which once seemed so bitter, knowing that His will is good and that, in His time and in His way, He is able to make the most bitter waters sweet.

RELINQUISHING CONTROL

Over the years, I have watched women walk through almost every conceivable ordeal, some of which have been unbelievably tragic or complex. I have prayed with friends through their struggles to cope with terminal disease, rebellious sons and daughters, abusive husbands, and torturous memories of sexual abuse. I have wept with women at the graveside of a little child, in the hospital following an accident that left their loved one on life support, and at the bedside of a husband dying from cancer.

Through those experiences I have learned a foundational truth. Whether the problem is earth-shattering or a mere blip on the radar screen of our lives, ultimately, the real issue is this: "Will I surrender to God's hand and purposes in my life?" Those who refuse to relinquish control become emotionally and spiritually bankrupt—bitter, demanding, impossible to live with. Those who say in simple surrender, "Yes, Lord," emerge from the experience spiritually rich, and their lives become a source of grace and encouragement to others who are hurting.

When we first enter into God's presence, it may be with the prayer, "O Lord, here's what I want: I wish You would remove this cup from me." Then as we wait before Him, we are reminded of the Son of God, who was asked to drink a bitter cup full of all the vilest sin of the world. He, too, asked that this cup might be removed from Him, that He might not have to drink it. But then He submitted His will to the will of the Father and chose the pathway of the cross, knowing that was what would please the Father. In the presence of such costly submission, our hearts are softened, our wills are bent, and we begin to pray, "O, my Father, not what I will, but what You will. If it pleases You, it pleases me."

WRESTLING WITH GOD

Jacob was a man with a godly heritage and a future bright with the promises of God. But he was a man who wanted it his way. In spite of momentary glimpses of God, he always seemed to be kicking against the boundaries—never content, always restless, always contending for that which God wanted to give him, but wanting to get it his way.

One day he came to a wall he couldn't move. In a matter of hours, he would have to face his twin brother, whom he had cheated years earlier and who was now coming to meet him accompanied by an army. For the first time in his life, Jacob couldn't manipulate his way around or out of a problem—which was exactly where God wanted him.

In the middle of the night, he finally got alone with the One who had been silently engineering all the circumstances of his life. Just Jacob and God. No one else around. In the stillness of that long night, Jacob wrestled for all he was worth. Like a child who keeps pressing an issue, but is really testing his parents to see if they will eventually give in, Jacob refused to give up the struggle, until finally, exhausted, he realized that he would never, ever be able to control God.

His will broken, his hip out of joint (don't expect to wrestle with God and come out unscathed), his name changed, Jacob emerged from that divine encounter a new man.

And so will we, when we finally get alone with God. In those precious (and sometimes painful) encounters, our lives will undergo a radical adjustment, in which our wills will become aligned with His. When we emerge, it will be to say with the Son of God, "I delight to do thy will, O my God" (Psalm 40:8 KJV).

Knowing the tendency of my heart to want its own will, I make it a practice to kneel before the Lord at least once each day. In doing so, I acknowledge that He is my Lord and I am His servant. As I bow before Him physically, my independent, stubborn, willful self bows to His absolute authority. I lay down any resistance, wave the white flag of surrender, and say in simple submission and worship, "Yes, Your Majesty."

Direction

I'm one of those people who have virtually no sense of direction. I recall one occasion when I left my hotel room, couldn't figure out where the elevator was, and had to stop and ask directions from one of the hotel employees in the hallway! Needless to say, I rely heavily on maps and written instructions to find just about everything.

Finding God's will regarding our lives, relationships, and responsibilities can be a lot trickier than finding a hotel elevator, a new restaurant, or a doctor's office. That's another important reason for spending time alone with Him on a consistent basis.

Remember: God wants to have an intimate relationship with us. One of the characteristics of an intimate friendship is the freedom to discuss any issue and to ask for the other's opinions or input on matters that concern us.

One of the things I value in my closest friends is the freedom to pick up the phone or get together, for the purpose of asking their input in areas where they have expertise or experience that I lack. I think of recent conversations in which I have asked for guidance on such practical matters as how to get my water softener fixed and how to know if my automobile and property insurance are providing the kind of coverage I need. In other conversations I have sought counsel on such matters as the hiring of a new staff member and whether I should accept a specific speaking engagement.

God desires to have the kind of relationship with us where we are quick to seek His counsel and direction in relation to the matters that concern us. His Word says, "If any of you lacks wisdom, he should ask God, who gives generously to all without finding fault, and it will be given to him" (James 1:5).

During our quiet time, we enter into His presence and lay our lives before Him—our schedules, our questions, and the circumstances and decisions we are facing. Then with His Word open before us and our hearts lifted up to Him, we listen and seek to discover His heart on the matter. We wait quietly before Him until He shines His light on our path.

There are so many matters where we need His guidance.

Take the matter of our schedule and priorities. I find that when I try to establish my own schedule—when I agree to meetings, appointments, and obligations without first seeking direction from the Lord—I end up with the frustration of having more to do than I can possibly handle, as well as being easily irritated by all those interruptions that put me farther behind.

However, I am learning to submit my calendar and daily schedule to the Lord, to ask Him before I make a commitment, to seek His will regarding my priorities, and to ask Him to order every aspect of my day (including the interruptions) according to His perfect will. Then, when those interruptions come (as they will), I can have the wisdom to know whether they are coming from His hand (in which case they are to be joyfully accepted) or whether they are to be avoided as an unnecessary distraction.

I've learned that there will never be enough time in the day for me to do everything on my "to do" list. There will never be time for me to do everything on everyone else's "to do" list for me. But there will always be enough time for me to do everything on *God's* "to do" list for my life.

That concept has helped release a lot of pressure in my schedule. On a regular basis, I ask the Lord to set me free from my own expectations and those of others and to help me discern what are *His* priorities for my life. Then I ask Him to give me the grace and the discipline to say yes only to that which He has ordered for me.

LEARNING TO LISTEN TO GOD

In recent years, I have been struck by how tuned and touch-sensitive Jesus was to the will of His Father. This particularly comes out in the gospel of John. Over and over again, Jesus spoke of doing the work His Father had sent Him to do. He refused to say anything that His Father had not told Him to say, to go anywhere that His Father had not told Him to go, or to do anything that His Father had not told Him to do (John 5:19, 30; 6:38; 7:16; 8:28; 12:49–50; 14:10). So committed was

He to pleasing His Father and to acting in one accord with Him, that He was unwilling to step out on His own and act independently.

But how did Jesus know what His priorities were to be on a given day, when there was a whole world to be redeemed? When there was a multitude of needy people standing at His feet, how did He know when to teach them and when to leave them in order to spend time with His disciples? How did He know who was the one woman in the crowd or the one leper by the side of the road that He was supposed to touch that day? How did He know how to handle each individual situation—whether He was to touch the blind man's eyes or simply to speak to him or to make mud and rub it on his eyes? How did He know that He was supposed to rebuke one group for their unbelief but encourage another man who admitted to struggling with doubts?

The answer takes us back to a discussion begun in chapter 1:

Very early in the morning, while it was still dark, Jesus got up, left the house and went off to a solitary place, where he prayed. (MARK 1:35)

He left the crowds long enough and regularly enough to say, "Father, what do *You* want me to do?"

At the end of this passage, Jesus' disciples go out working for Him. "Lord," they say, "everyone is looking for You." Jesus' activities of the preceding day are on the front page of every major newspaper. He's the most popular program in town. This is a press agent's dream! But Jesus says, "We're not going to stay here; we're going on to the next town."

"But, Jesus, why? We could stay booked here for at least another month! There are so many people who need You here. Why move on?"

"Because that's what My Father wants Me to do."

How did He know? Because He got quiet enough, long enough, to listen to His Father's heart.

Some of us have no clue what God wants us to do with

our lives or with our days. We can't figure out how to resolve conflicts in our homes, how to meet the needs of those closest to us, how to reach our neighbors with the gospel, or how to make simple decisions. The reason may be that we have not sat still long enough to ask Him for direction.

HOW GOD SPEAKS

God directs us through His Word. As we read and meditate on the Word, the indwelling Spirit illuminates it to our understanding and gives us the wisdom to know how it applies to specific, practical areas of our lives. He uses His Word to reveal His priorities to us.

There are many good activities that simply are not God's priorities for this season of our lives. So when someone comes and says, "Will you teach a Sunday school class?" or "sing in the choir" or "baby-sit for my children" or "take over this new project for the company" or whatever, what do you do? You say, "Let me check with the Lord first, and I'll let you know."

But, you wonder, how do I "check with the Lord"? Will He actually tell me whether or not I should teach that Sunday school class or take on the new project? Probably not. But what He will do is use His Word and His Spirit to direct your steps.

I often claim the promise of Proverbs 16:3 (KJV): "Commit thy works unto the LORD, and thy thoughts shall be established." As I am praying regarding a specific decision or issue, I will sometimes symbolically place that concern in my hands, then lift my cupped hands up to the Lord and say, "Lord, I am committing this matter to You. I am Your servant; I want to do what You want me to do. Please establish my thoughts and use Your Word to guide me to a wise decision that will please You."

God may bring to mind various Scriptures that have bearing on the situation—perhaps something about priorities, values, attitudes, or responses. He may impress me to seek counsel from a godly individual or a spiritual authority. He may remind me of another priority He has already given me that I would have to violate to take on a new task. Or He may grant the desire, the faith, and the freedom in my heart to step out in a new venture.

The Scripture says, "In your light we see light" (Psalm 36:9). And "the entrance of thy words giveth light" (Psalm 119:130 KJV). Do you need light for your pathway? Do you need direction for how to raise that child for whom no textbook was ever written? how to deal with a husband who is addicted to pornography? how to respond to that overbearing fellow employee? how to encourage a friend who is going through a crisis? how to care for an aging parent with Alzheimer's? How do you get direction? "The entrance of thy words giveth light."

INQUIRING OF GOD

Second Chronicles 20 tells the familiar story of a vast army of Moabites and Ammonites that came together to make war against Judah. We read that King Jehoshaphat was alarmed and "resolved to inquire of the LORD" (v. 3). Before calling a meeting of the National Defense Council, he called a solemn assembly for the people to come and fast and seek the Lord. In his prayer, Jehoshaphat laid out the facts before the Lord. He closed his prayer by saying, "We do not know what to do, but our eyes are upon you" (v. 12). In answer to that prayer, God dramatically and decisively defeated the enemy, using one of the most unusual battle plans in history.

Many years later, the king of Assyria sent the commander of his army to Jerusalem to publicly humiliate and threaten King Hezekiah (2 Kings 18:17–35). When Hezekiah received news of the incident, he sent messengers to the prophet Isaiah to ask him to pray (19:1–4). Isaiah did pray and the crisis was averted. However, a short time later, the king of Assyria sent another intimidating message to Hezekiah. What was Hezekiah to do? I love his response:

Hezekiah received the letter from the messengers and read it. Then he went up to the temple of the LORD and spread it out before the LORD. And Hezekiah prayed to the LORD. (2 KINGS 19:14–15)

What is the crisis, the difficulty, the decision you are facing? Spread it out before the Lord, and pray:

> *Lead me, O Lord, in your righteousness . . .*
> *make straight your way before me.*
> —PSALM 5:8

Then stand back and watch as He directs your steps. The Good Shepherd promises to guide His sheep in "paths of righteousness" (Psalm 23:3). Believe His Word; He will not fail you.

ntercession

Another purpose of spending time alone with the Lord is that we might intercede on behalf of the needs of others. As we linger in His presence, we find Him to be a "friend closer than a brother," a Good Shepherd, a loving Father who delights to meet the needs of His children. We drink deeply from the well of His love and goodness until our own souls are full and satisfied. We look into His face and find grace and acceptance. We listen to His heart, learn of His ways, and receive His provision and direction for our lives.

Now there comes to our mind a friend who is in need. We would gladly meet that need out of our own supply, if we could. But our meager resources are not sufficient for our friend's great need. Then we remember that there is One whose supply never runs out and who delights to give good gifts to His children. And so we are emboldened to approach Him on behalf of those we love.

We go to His door and knock. When He delays coming to the door, we continue knocking, appealing earnestly for our friend in need, until He comes and grants our request. This is what Andrew Murray referred to as "the threefold cord that cannot be broken: the hungry friend needing the help, the praying friend seeking the help, and the Mighty Friend, loving to give as much as he needeth"[1] (see Luke 11:5–13).

In that quiet time alone with the Lord, we come boldly and humbly to His throne of grace to obtain mercy, not only for ourselves, but for those He has entrusted to our care and whose needs weigh heavily on us, and to plead for grace to help them in their time of need.

As those four men in Jesus' day tore a hole in the roof to bring their paralytic friend to the Master (Mark 2:1–5), so we press through whatever barriers of helplessness, doubt, or fear may be in our way, in order to lift our friends up to His throne, knowing that He alone can meet their need. There we say, "O Lord, You have done so much for me. Now I come to You again, not for some need of my own—You have abundantly met my needs—but for this one that I love, asking You to reach down and touch his life, to make him whole, to woo his heart, to remove the blinders from his eyes, to grant him strength for this hour of testing, to place Your guardian angels round his heart and home, to loose him from the chains of impurity and rebellion . . ."

"HAVE YOU PRAYED ABOUT IT?"

Most of us are born "fixers." Our natural tendency is to take matters into our own hands, to fret and worry, and to demand solutions. In the process, we often bypass the one truly effective means we have of impacting the lives of those around us. A little plaque on my desk reads, "Have you prayed about it?" Unfortunately, I often overlook that simple question until I have already exhausted all my own ideas and solutions.

I am convinced that if you and I would spend a fraction of the time praying about our concerns for others that we do worrying about them, talking about them to others, and trying to fix them ourselves, we would see a whole lot more results. Sometimes I picture God sitting up in heaven, watching us frantically trying to manage everyone else's lives and solve their problems. Then I hear Him saying, "Do you want to take care of this? Go ahead. Oh, you want *Me* to handle it? Well, let Me show you what I can do!" The hymn writer was right when he said:

> O what peace we often forfeit,
> O what needless pain we bear,
> All because we do not carry
> Everything to God in prayer!
>
> —JOSEPH M. SCRIVEN (1819–86)

In his wonderful little book *With Christ in the School of Prayer,* Andrew Murray points us to the example of Abraham:

> In Abraham we see how prayer is not only, or even chiefly, the means of obtaining blessing for ourselves, but is the exercise of his royal prerogative to influence the destinies of men, and the will of God which rules them. We do not once find Abraham praying for himself. His prayer for Sodom and Lot, for Abimelech, for Ishmael, prove what power a man, who is God's friend, has to make the history of those around him.[2]

So many of us live in the realm of the natural. We have only seen what our natural ability and effort can do. Have you found yourself trying to change your coworker, your husband, your children, your pastor, your friends? Has it worked? How about letting God work on them!

Recently a woman approached me during a conference and shared that, for many years, she had tried to change her husband. When she heard me speak a year earlier, God had said to her, "Why don't you let Me change you first?" Tenderly, she told me how she had allowed God to work in her life, and then, how she had released her husband to God and begun to really pray for him. With tears of joy in her eyes, she said, "He's not the same man today that he was a year ago!"

Why are we so slow to believe what God can do? Is there someone you have been trying to change? A situation in someone else's life that you have been trying to "fix"? Your truest Friend invites you to bring that needy person to the throne of grace. Enter into His presence and say, "O Lord, I can't meet this child's need; I can't change this person; I can't solve this problem or fix this situation. But I know that nothing is too difficult for You. Please give me wisdom; show me how to be the friend, the wife, the mother, the employee that You want me to be. Please intervene in this person's life; draw him to Yourself."

God does not promise to eliminate all our problems or to change all the difficult people in our lives. But He does promise to listen to the cries of His children and to act in accordance with His holy, eternal purposes.

Transformation

We come now to a final purpose of spending time alone with God. Perhaps it is the most glorious of all. For as we linger in His presence, we are transformed into His likeness.

We have heard it said that couples who have been married for many years start to look like each other. I don't know how it happens, but in many cases it seems to be true.

The fact is, we become like the people we spend time with. We begin to take on the characteristics of the people and things on which we focus. For example, a woman who becomes obsessed with a critical, controlling mother-in-law faces the danger of becoming a critical, controlling woman herself. How important it is, then, that we fix our eyes on the One whose image we wish to bear.

We saw earlier how Moses spent concentrated hours and days alone in the presence of God. The Scripture tells us that when Moses came down from receiving God's Law on Mount Sinai, "he was not aware that his face was radiant because he had spoken with the LORD" (Exodus 34:29). The radiance was the manifest glory of God being reflected from Moses' face. The passage goes on to say that *when Moses finished speaking to them, he put a veil over his face. But whenever he entered the LORD'S presence to speak with him, he removed the veil until he came out. And when he came out and told the Israelites what he had been commanded, they saw that his face was radiant. Then Moses would put the veil back over his face until he went in to speak with the LORD. (EXODUS 34:33–35)*

METAMORPHOSIS OR MASQUERADE?

When the apostle Paul wrote to the Corinthians, he referred to this account and explained its significance for our lives. He compared the glory of the old covenant, which faded away and ministered condemnation and death, to the far superior glory of the new covenant, which gives life and will never fade away. Then he explained that, as Moses gazed upon the glory of God with an unveiled face and was transformed, so "we, who with unveiled faces all contemplate [marginal reading] the Lord's glory, are being transformed into His likeness with ever-increasing glory, which comes from the Lord" (2 Corinthians 3:18).

To me, this is one of the most wondrous verses in all of God's Word. Paul is saying that as we come into God's presence, without masks or pretense, but with our lives open and exposed before Him, and as we steadfastly gaze on Him, we will gradually take on His likeness—we will be transformed.

The word translated "transformed" ("changed," KJV) is the Greek word *metamorphoō*, the word from which we get our English word "metamorphose." It suggests a complete change that takes place from the inside out, much as a caterpillar is metamorphosed into a butterfly. Besides the passage in 2 Corinthians 3, this word is used in only two other instances in the New Testament. It is used in the Gospels to describe what took place on the Mount of Transfiguration, as Jesus prayed (Luke 9:29) and He was *"transfigured* before them. His face shone like the sun, and his clothes became as white as the light" (Matthew 17:2, emphasis added; see also Mark 9:2). It is used again in Romans 12:2, where Paul says that we are not to be

conformed to this world, but rather, we are to be "transformed" by the renewing of our minds.

In contrast to being transformed, we read in 2 Corinthians
11:13–14 of "false apostles, deceitful workmen, masquerading
as apostles of Christ," and of Satan himself, who "masquer-
ades as an angel of light." The word translated "masquerade" is
the Greek word, *metaschēmatizō*, which speaks of change that is
merely outward—simply a change of appearance.

This second word is one we could use to describe children
who ring our doorbell on Halloween, masquerading as clowns
or pirates. Those children are not really clowns or pirates—
they are just wearing a mask or a costume that makes them
appear to be something other than what they really are.

The sad fact is that many of us as believers are merely
masquerading as "good Christians." Inwardly, we are not like
Christ at all—we are selfish, lazy, bitter, and angry. But we want
everyone to think we are like Jesus, so we put on our "good
Christian" masks—especially when we get to church.

That's a bit like sticking oranges to the branches of a lemon
tree and calling it an orange tree. It may look like an orange
tree, but it's still a lemon tree.

God doesn't want us to masquerade. He wants us to be
metamorphosed—to be transformed from the inside out into
the likeness of the Lord Jesus. We can masquerade in the energy of our own flesh but are likely to end up frazzled and frustrated. Only the Spirit of God can metamorphose (transform)
us into the image of Jesus.

How does that glorious process take place? As we "behold
Him with an unveiled face," as we gaze steadfastly upon His
likeness, we will become like Him, by the power of His Holy
Spirit. As you begin spending time each day looking into the
face of Jesus, beholding Him, and listening to His voice, you
will find that your life will be transfigured from the inside out.
You will begin to think as He thinks, to love as He loves, and to
obey His voice, as He obeyed the will of His Father.

Do you want to be a gracious, kind, loving, sweet-spirited

woman? You can be, and you will be, as you are transformed in His presence.

And when will that process be complete? When we finally see Him face-to-face, "we shall be like him, for we shall see him as he is" (1 John 3:2).

TRANSFORMED BY LOVE

In the Old Testament book called the Song of Solomon (or Song of Songs), we read the story of a wealthy king who decides to find a bride. Much to everyone's surprise, the king does not pick one of the wealthy, well-educated, well-bred young women of the city. Rather, he goes out into the country and selects a common, ordinary peasant girl to be his bride. She is not beautiful; in fact, her skin is rough and dark from having worked out in the sun in her family's vineyards. When the king brings her back to the palace, the "daughters of Jerusalem" are astonished at his choice. And no one is more astonished than the girl herself.

Nonetheless, the king takes his bride into his bedchamber, where he lavishes his love on her. By the end of the story, this young peasant girl has become a lovely, radiant woman whose beauty attracts the attention of all who see her. What has happened? She has spent time alone with her bridegroom. And she has taken on his characteristics. It is not her own loveliness, but his, that others see in her. She has been transformed by his love.

Deep within the heart of every true child of God is a longing to be like Jesus, to reflect His beauty. We cry out,

> O to be like Thee! O to be like Thee,
>   Blessed Redeemer, pure as Thou art!
> Come in Thy sweetness, come in Thy fulness —
>   Stamp Thine own image deep on my heart.
> —THOMAS O. CHISHOLM (1866–1960)

But there are no shortcuts to Christlikeness. Shortcuts only

lead to masquerading. There is no substitute for spending consistent, quality time alone in His presence. The cost is great. But
the rewards are even greater. If we want to be transformed, we
must be willing to

> Take time to be holy, speak oft with thy Lord;
>   Abide in Him always, and feed on His Word. . . .
> Take time to be holy, the world rushes on;
>   Much time spend in secret with Jesus alone;
> By looking to Jesus, like Him thou shalt be;
>   Thy friends in thy conduct His likeness shall
>   see.
>
> —WILLIAM D. LONGSTAFF (1822–94)

MAKING IT PERSONAL

1. Have you found yourself resisting God's choices or will in any area of your life? Identify the specific issue. Will you choose right now to wave the white flag of surrender and submit your will to His? You may wish to bow physically before Him as an expression of submission; then verbalize your surrender in words something like these: "Yes, Your Majesty; I receive this as from Your hand. Use it to mold and make me into the image of Jesus."

2. Is there a matter of current concern that is pressing in on you? Why not "spread it out" before the Lord, as Hezekiah did with the threatening letter from the king of Assyria? Find some tangible symbol of that problem (for example, a letter, photograph, contract, checkbook, journal entry, or marriage license), lay it before the Lord, and ask Him to give you wisdom, to direct your steps, to meet the need, and to bring glory to Himself through the situation.

3. Record the name of a friend or family member who has a great need at this time. Write a brief summary of his or her specific need(s). Then commit yourself to intercede on that person's behalf every day for the next thirty days.

4 Make a list of qualities in the life of Jesus that you want to be true in your life. Ask God to transform you into His likeness by the power of His Word and His Spirit.

░░░ FROM THE HEART OF ░░░

Mary Madeline Whittinghill

A consistent devotional life feeds my soul as food does my body. It fine-tunes me to God's heart and ways, and enables me to keep short accounts with Him and others. It helps me to walk in dependence on Him. As a friend says, "It sets my sails for the day."

I used to come up with a lofty plan for spending one to two hours with the Lord every morning. When many obstacles sabotaged that goal, I was tempted to feel that if I couldn't do it all, then to spend only thirty minutes wouldn't be of value.

I have a different perspective now. I will plan for blocks of time with the Lord in the early mornings, benefit from what He gives, and always hunger for more. To hear from God personally, worship Him, and seek Him on behalf of others is my delight. If my time is cut short, I try to continue in that same attitude of prayer throughout the day. The "daily" is more important than the length.

When our five children were younger, I didn't manage the consistency I longed for. If I had to do it over, I would set smaller, more realistic goals, and let the Lord increase the time when possible. I realize that quantity of time is not the key factor; but I also know that it takes time to worship, pray, intercede, and pore over God's Word.

I love to begin by reading a short devotional, followed by singing hymns, psalms, and other worship songs. Then I read a passage of Scripture, seeking to listen to God's voice, and pray it in. An important ingredient is confession of sin and being sensitive to ways God wants to teach and change me. I have begun journaling lately, which has been a real blessing and has given added focus and clarity.

Then, with a clean heart, I intercede for others. Praying aloud helps keep my thoughts from wandering. It is helpful to have a prayer journal with a focused plan for praying for the people and needs the Lord brings our way. I know I can't pray for every person and need every day, so I ask the Lord to bring to mind those who need special prayer that day.

□ □ □ --

Mary Madeline Whittinghill is a homeschool mom and the wife of evangelist Al Whittinghill. She and Al have five children and have served with Precept Ministries and Ambassadors for Christ.

NOTES

1. Andrew Murray, *With Christ in the School of Prayer* (London: James Nisbet, 1886), 61.

2. Ibid., 135.

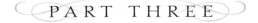

PART THREE

The Pattern of a Devotional Life

Very early in the morning, while it was still dark, Jesus got up.

MARK 1:35

The morning watch is essential. You must not face the day until you have faced God, nor look into the face of others until you have looked into His.

You cannot expect to be victorious if the day begins only in your own strength. Face the work of every day with the influence of a few thoughtful, quiet moments with your heart and God. Do not meet other people, even those of your own home, until you have first met the great Guest and honored Companion of your life—Jesus Christ.

Meet Him alone. Meet Him regularly. Meet Him with His open Book of counsel before you; and face the regular and irregular duties of each day with the influence of His personality definitely controlling your every act.

STREAMS IN THE DESERT

CHAPTER 5

Getting Started

OK, you say. I see the importance of spending time alone with God. I really want to begin making this the number one priority in my life. I want to cultivate a relationship with God and walk in intimate union and communion with Him. I want to be transformed into the image of Christ. But . . . how do I get started?

In this chapter, we will look at three general principles in relation to establishing a personal devotional life. Each of these principles is taught in the Scripture and illustrated in the life of the Lord Jesus. Then, in the chapters that follow, we will examine a number of specific ingredients that are an important part of our time alone with God.

A Consistent Practice

Jesus often withdrew.
LUKE 5:16

The first general principle is one we have seen earlier in

this book. Jesus made time alone with His Father a consistent part of His daily schedule—and so must we. Moreover, these daily devotions are not just an obligation for us, but an incredible privilege—the very God of the universe wants to meet with *us*.

In his penetrating book *Spiritual Disciplines for the Christian Life*, Donald Whitney issues this winsome invitation:

> Think of it: The Lord Jesus Christ is willing to meet with you privately for as long as you want, and He is willing—even eager—to meet with you every day! Suppose you had been one of the thousands who followed Jesus around for much of the last three years of His earthly life. Can you imagine how excited you would have been if one of His disciples said, "The Master wants us to tell you that He is willing to get alone with you whenever you're willing, and for as much time as you want to spend, and He'll be expecting you most every day"? What a privilege! Who would have complained about this expectation? Well, that marvelous privilege and expectation is always yours.[1]

I have had the joy of walking with God since early childhood. I have been blessed to have grown up in a godly home, to have received fourteen years of Christian education, to have been exposed to the lives of many godly men and women, and to have sat under some of the best Bible teachers of our generation.

But I have come to believe that it is absolutely impossible for me to cultivate an intimate relationship with God or to become the woman He wants me to be, apart from spending *daily* time alone with Him. I cannot set aside time for God sporadically, whenever I am able to squeeze Him into my schedule, and hope to enjoy a vital, growing friendship with Him. That isn't possible in human relationships, and it is no more possible in our relationship with God.

A DAILY SUPPLY

The Old Testament provides us with a number of illustrations of the necessity of meeting with God on a daily basis.

During the forty years that the children of Israel wandered in the wilderness, en route from Egypt to the Promised Land, God provided for all of their needs—sometimes in unusual ways. He met their physical need for bread by sending manna—"thin flakes like frost on the ground [that] appeared on the desert floor" (Exodus 16:14). How often did He send the manna? Every day (except for the Sabbath). And how often did the people have to gather the manna? Every day. Six days a week, fifty-two weeks a year, for forty years. Notice that every person had to gather his own portion (v. 16). Nobody else could gather it for him. God gave exactly what was needed for each individual to have his needs met for that day.

This physical bread was a picture of the Bread of Life—the Word of God. God created both our bodies and our souls to require daily sustenance. He reminded His people that "man does not live on bread alone but on every word that comes from the mouth of the Lord" (Deuteronomy 8:3). Physical nourishment was not sufficient—they needed spiritual nourishment, as well. Just as they needed to gather and eat physical bread on a daily basis, so they needed to gather and partake of the Bread of Life to feed their souls on a daily basis.

When Jesus taught us to pray, "Give us this day our daily bread," He was not only teaching us to trust God to supply our daily physical needs, but He was also reminding us of the importance of seeking from Him the spiritual nourishment that our souls need each day.

D. L. Moody said, "A man can no more take in a supply of grace for the future than he can eat enough for the next six months, or take sufficient air into his lungs at one time to sustain life for a week. We must draw upon God's boundless store of grace from day to day as we need it."[2] That store of grace is made available to us one day at a time, and the manna in the wilderness reminds us of our need to gather it up for ourselves one day at a time.

DAILY ROUTINES

In the tabernacle, there was another reminder of the need to cultivate daily union and communion with God. At the entrance to the Holy of Holies stood the altar of incense. God told Moses:

Aaron must burn fragrant incense on the altar every morning when he tends the lamps. He must burn incense again when he lights the lamps at twilight so incense will burn regularly before the LORD. (EXODUS 30:7–8)

The incense that was offered on this altar spoke of the praise and prayers of a redeemed people ascending up to God. It was to be offered up, not occasionally, or whenever the priest happened to think of it, but every day—every morning and every night. Why did it matter to God if they occasionally missed a day or two? Because He was pursuing a relationship with His people. And He knew that required consistent, daily communication. It was this incense that the high priest carried with him when he entered into the Holy of Holies once a year on the Day of Atonement. And so we are invited to enter into His holy presence, taking with us the incense of praise and prayer regularly offered up to God.

There were other regular routines that took place in the tabernacle. The oil lamps had to be kept burning continually, sacrifices had to be made, the showbread had to be replaced, and the priests had to be cleansed. Every morning, every evening, day in, day out.

You say, That could become a meaningless routine. You're right. In fact, that's exactly what happened to the Israelites. They lost sight of the purpose behind the routines—to walk in union and communion with their God. But the routines were still right. They were established by God. And they were necessary to sustain a relationship with Him.

Of course, there's always a danger that a daily quiet time or any other spiritual discipline can deteriorate into a lifeless routine. But I have discovered that it is much easier to breathe life back into a dead routine than to get life where there is no routine at all.

THE BRIDEGROOM DESIRES HIS BRIDE

As you seek to set aside time each day to meet with God, don't forget that the objective is to cultivate an intimate relationship between you and God. He longs for such a relationship with you, and He is eager to spend that time with you.

There is a touching moment in the Song of Solomon when the king bids his bride to leave what she is doing and join him, so they can spend some intimate time alone together. "Rise up, my love, my fair one, and come away," he calls to her from outside the window. "Let me see thy countenance, let me hear thy voice; for sweet is thy voice, and thy countenance is comely" (Song of Solomon 2:10, 14 KJV).

This passage has radically altered my perspective on the whole matter of daily devotions and helped me see that my heavenly Bridegroom longs to spend time with me. Time with Him is not just something that *I* need (though I do need Him desperately); it is something that fulfills a longing in *His* heart. When I go into His presence in the morning, it is with a need and a desire to see His face and to hear His voice. But have you ever stopped to realize that He wants to see *your* face and hear *your* voice?

That was an astonishing thought to me. My heart said in wonder and amazement, "Lord, why would *You* want to see *my* face? What could you possibly see in me that would bless You? Why would You want to hear *my* voice? What could I possibly say that would minister to Your heart?" After all these years of walking with Him, I still cannot fathom why He would want to meet with me. But I know it is true. So when I enter into His presence, it is with the thought that He wants to be with me, and that I can bring Him pleasure by letting Him look on me and letting Him hear my voice.

A song by Larnelle Harris and Phil McHugh points out the

fact that when we neglect our time with Him, there are *two* people who feel the effect. Not only is *our* spirit left dry and empty; but *His* heart is grieved:

> There He was just waiting in our old familiar place;
> An empty spot beside Him where I once used to wait
> To be filled with strength and wisdom for the battles of
>   the day.
> I would have passed Him by again, but I clearly heard Him
>   say,
> I miss My time with you, those moments together.
> I need to be with you each day, and it hurts me when you
>   say
> You're too busy, busy tryin' to serve Me.
> But how can you serve Me, when your spirit's empty?
> There's a longing in My heart, wanting more than just a
>   part of you.
> It's true; I miss my time with you.[3]

When it comes down to it, spending time with God is more necessary than anything else you or I do on a daily basis, including eating, sleeping, getting dressed, and going to work.

At this particular season of your life (and remember that seasons do change), you may not be able to spend uninterrupted hours alone with the Lord each day. But if knowing God and having a relationship with Him is important to you, you can and will determine to set aside *some* time each day to listen to Him and to let Him know that you love Him and need Him.

In the Morning

Very early in the morning, while it was still dark.
MARK 1:35

Just as Jesus made time alone with His Father a consistent

part of His daily schedule and bids us to do the same, so also He bids us rise early for those devotions. This point has already been made at several places in this book, but it is so important it needs to be emphasized here. Whenever the subject of daily devotions comes up, "in the morning" seems to be the point that evokes the most frustration, and even resistance, especially among mothers. I have often been tempted to minimize or skip over this point. But the more I study the Word and the ways of God, the more convinced I am of the importance of starting the day with Him. The scriptural case for a morning watch is hard to refute. Listen to these verses (emphasis added):

> *My voice shalt thou hear* in the morning, O LORD; in the morning *will I direct my prayer unto thee, and will look up.*

> *I cry to you for help, O LORD;*
>   in the morning *my prayer comes before you.*

> *Awake, my soul!*
>   *Awake, harp and lyre!*
>   I will awaken the dawn.
> I will praise You, O Lord.

> *I rise* before dawn *and cry for help;*
>   I have put my hope in your word.

> *Cause me to hear thy lovingkindness* in the morning.

> *He wakens me* morning by morning,
>   wakens my ear to listen like one being taught.
>   —PSALM 5:3 KJV; PSALMS 88:13; 57:8–9; 119:147;
>   PSALM 143:8 KJV; ISAIAH 50:4

Jacob rose early in the morning to make a vow to God at Bethel (Genesis 28:18–19).

God said to Moses, "Be ready *in the morning*, and come up *in the morning* unto mount Sinai, and present thyself there to me" (Exodus 34:2 KJV, emphasis added).

David rose early in the morning for worship, prayer, and meditation.

Early on that first Easter Sunday morning, Mary Magdalene and the other Mary went to the tomb where Jesus had been buried (Matthew 28:1).

God sent manna for His people *in the morning*. The day's supply of nourishment was to be gathered *in the morning*, while it was still fresh. Every morning God has a fresh store of mercies available for His people. When we do not turn aside in the morning to gather what He has provided for that day, we are saying, in essence, I can make it through this day on my own. My strength, my wisdom, my resources are sufficient for the demands of this day. Not only do we forfeit the grace of God, but our self-sufficiency and pride force Him to resist us throughout the day.

You may be wondering, *How early* in the morning do I need to meet with God? I don't know what time early is for you. Since my office is in my home, early for me is before the phone begins to ring. If I have not met with God by that time, it becomes almost impossible for me to find a quiet time, a quiet place, or a quiet heart for the rest of the day. After that point, I have lost the most precious, valuable time of the day and my quiet time will generally be fragmented, at best.

That doesn't mean that in order to be spiritual you have to be one of those women who just loves mornings and bounds out of bed two hours before the sun comes up. Neither am I suggesting a legalistic, ironclad approach that says if you're not on your knees by five o'clock in the morning, you're not spiritual. Don't forget that the purpose is to know God and to have a relationship with Him. But the bottom line is, if you and I want to be like Jesus, if we want to really know God, we have got to be willing to pay the price to get out of bed in the morning to seek His face.

Men of God throughout history have stressed the importance of meeting God in the morning. Listen to the unison
urging of these spiritual greats:

> Begin the day with God!
>   He is thy Sun and Day!
> His is the radiance of thy dawn
>   To Him address thy day.
>
> Sing thy first song to God!
>   Not to thy fellow men;
> Not to the creatures of His hand,
>   But to the glorious One.
>
> —HORATIUS BONAR (1808–89)[4]

Do not have your concert first and tune your instruments after-
ward. Begin the day with God. (J. HUDSON TAYLOR)

It is a good rule never to look into the face of man in the morning till you have looked into the face of God. (CHARLES H. SPUR-
GEON)[5]

The best time to converse with God is before worldly occasion
stands knocking at the door to be let in: the morning is, as it
were, the cream of the day; let the cream be taken off, and let
God have it. Wind up thy heart towards heaven in the beginning
of the day, and it will go the better all the day after. He that los-
eth his heart in the morning in the world, will hardly find it
again all the day. (THOMAS WATSON)[6]

One of the things I have learned over the years is that success in meeting God in the morning begins the night before.
Each evening we make choices that determine whether or not
we can get up in the morning. One of the reasons my father
was able to be so consistent at spending at least an hour with
God early each morning was that he was disciplined about
getting to bed on time the night before. Regardless of what
else was going on in our home, no later than ten o'clock he

would excuse himself and prepare to be in bed by eleven.

Today we children laugh affectionately when we recall hearing him say to guests, "Good night! Be sure to lock the door and turn out the lights when you leave." He did not communicate a rigid or uptight spirit about this discipline. He simply wanted to be sure he didn't miss the most important meeting of his day—an early morning meeting with the most important Person in his life.

I might mention that the absence of a television in our home did a lot to assist in this commitment to get to bed at night. Rather than staying up at night to listen to the eleven o'-clock news, followed by *Nightline*, followed by . . . , how much better off would our souls be if we got to bed earlier and spent the last portion of our evening listening to godly music or meditating on Scripture—preparing for our morning appointment with God.

By the way, moms, you cannot fathom the impact it will have on your children, for them to know when they awaken that you have already met with the Lord—that you have prayed for them and committed all the day's activities to the Lord. To this day, whenever I am tempted to hit my day running, as is often the case, I have the image of a mother and father who set the pattern of spending time with the Lord before conducting any other business of the day.

Over the years, God has used this familiar poem to remind me of the importance of meeting Him in the morning:

> I met God in the morning
>> When my day was at its best,
> And His presence came like sunrise,
>> Like a glory in my breast.
>
> All day long the presence lingered,
>> All day long, He stayed with me,
> And we sailed in perfect calmness
>> O'er a very troubled sea.

Other lives were blown and battered,
 Other lives were sore distressed,
But the winds that seemed to drive them
 Bring to us a peace and rest.
Then I thought of other mornings,
 With a keen remorse of mind,
When I too had loosed the moorings,
 With the presence left behind.

So I think I know the secret,
 Learned from many a troubled way:
You must seek Him in the morning,
 If you want Him through the day!
 —RALPH SPAULDING CUSHMAN[7]

A Solitary Place

Jesus went out to a solitary place.
LUKE 4:42

In order to cultivate intimacy, husbands and wives need to spend time alone with each other—away from friends, acquaintances, and even their own children.

Jesus understood the importance of getting away from the crowd in order to sustain an intimate relationship with His Father. Luke 5:15 tells us that when news about Him spread, "crowds of people came to hear him and to be healed of their sicknesses." Jesus had compassion on the multitudes and gave of Himself sacrificially to minister to their needs. But He knew He could not meet their needs if He did not draw upon His relationship with His Father. So the very next verse tells us that Jesus often "withdrew to *lonely places* and prayed" (5:16, emphasis added).

When God called Moses up to meet with Him on Mount Sinai, He said, "Present yourself to me there on top of the mountain. No one is to come with you" (Exodus 34:2–3). As part of a community of faith, we need times to worship, pray, and seek the Lord in the company of God's people. But we must also have times that are set apart to be alone with Him. There are dimensions to our relationship with God that cannot be nurtured and sustained in a crowd.

A TENT OF MEETING

Before the tabernacle was constructed, the Scripture says that Moses used to take a tent and pitch it outside the camp some distance away, calling it the "tent of meeting." Anyone inquiring of the Lord would go to the tent of meeting outside the camp (Exodus 33:7). This special meeting place was set up away from the crowd, away from the normal flow of traffic. It was a set-apart place, a place reserved for meeting with God.

I have found it helpful to set apart in my home a place for meeting with God. In one corner of my study sits a comfortable chair on a slightly raised platform. That chair has become my quiet time chair. It is my tent of meeting—a place where I go to meet with God. Because I travel a great deal, I am not always able to meet with God in the same place. But wherever I may be, I seek to establish a tent of meeting in my heart—a quiet place, a solitary place, a place away from the crowd, a place where I can be alone with God.

A mother with several children may find it difficult to find a solitary place. A pastor's wife wrote and shared how she managed to withdraw from the crowd:

> I have a sweet memory of our son, Jon, when he was approximately 18 months old. He would get out of his baby bed each morning, coming to find me. The only place in our small house where I could be away from the children (ages 8, 6, 2, and 1) was in our small bathroom with a sliding door. Of course, there was only one place to sit in the bathroom. So, with the lid down and my Bible open I'd have my quiet time. Jon would come outside the door, put his little hand under the door, and hold onto my

foot until I finished. At that early age, he had learned that I had to read my Bible daily.

A friend with small children once said to me, "There have been times when we have been visiting relatives and I've had to have my quiet time by a night-light, in the same room where my children were sleeping. But I've found that there's a way to do it, if you really want to."

Your tent of meeting may be a bathroom, a closet, a hallway, or even an automobile. The important thing is that you find a place where you can meet *alone* with your heavenly Bridegroom.

If your temperament is anything like mine, you may find it difficult to get used to solitude. Particularly if you are accustomed to having the television or the radio on all the time, or to always being around other people, it can be an adjustment to find yourself quiet and alone with God. But, as one writer reminds us:

> There is a strange strength conceived in solitude. Crows go in flocks and wolves in packs, but the lion and the eagle are solitaires. Strength is not in bluster and noise. . . .
>
> Strength is in quietness. The lake must be calm if the heavens are to be reflected on its surface. Our Lord loved the people, but how often we read of His going away from them for a brief season. . . .
>
> The one thing needed above all others today is that we shall go apart with our Lord, and sit at His feet in the sacred privacy of His blessed presence. Oh, for the lost art of meditation! Oh, for the culture of the secret place! Oh, for the tonic of waiting upon God![8]

A PERSONAL TESTIMONY
(One "Happy Meal" to Go, Please!)

From the time I was twenty, for nearly twelve years, I traveled full-time, year-round. During that period, I became a fast-food junkie. More times than I care to remember, I picked up my tacos or burger and fries at the drive-through window, and then would sit in the parking lot for the two and a half minutes it took to inhale my meal. Frequently, I didn't even bother to stop, but would just keep right on going, eating my lunch while driving to the next appointment.

I actually didn't mind living that way—until I reached the age of thirty. About that time, my body started to feel the effects of years of junk food. I found that my body was craving a more nutritious, balanced diet, and that I couldn't keep eating the way I had for over a decade. I had to make some fairly drastic changes in my lifestyle to accommodate my body's needs.

A number of years ago, after going through an eighteen-month period in which my schedule had been unusually grueling, I woke up one day and realized that I had become a *spiritual* fast-food junkie. I had allowed deadlines, projects, and demands to take priority over my relationship with the Lord. Oh, I still had a quiet time—of sorts. I usually managed to get in some sort of spiritual meal. But all too frequently, that meal had come to consist of hurriedly reading a short passage of Scripture just before running out the door to accomplish one more thing for God.

Spiritually, I was living in fast-food drive-throughs. I was having my devotions, if you could call it that. But I wasn't having *devotion*. I wasn't meeting with God. I wasn't nurturing our relationship.

Like the Shulammite bride in the Song of Solomon, I had tended the vineyards of others—I had been busy tending to everyone else's well-being, but I had failed to tend the garden of my own heart (Song of Solomon 1:6).

As God used circumstances to reveal my malnourished spiritual condition, I began to realize what a price I had paid for those months of neglect.

How grateful I am for a merciful, long-suffering heavenly Father who never stops pursuing a love relationship with those who belong to Him. Graciously, kindly, He wooed my heart that had become so distracted and desensitized to Him. His goodness led me to repent of having wandered so far from His side, to renew my vows to Him, and to reestablish my relationship with Him as the number one priority of my day. As I responded to His initiative, the Good Shepherd began the process of restoring my soul, leading me to the still waters and green pastures that I so desperately needed.

In the Song of Solomon we are told of an instance when the bride, through failure to respond to the initiative of her Bridegroom, experienced a loss of intimacy. Troubled by the breach in the relationship, she set out on an intense search for her Beloved. In recounting that thrilling moment when He was restored to her, she says, "I found him whom my soul loveth: I held him, and would not let him go" (Song of Solomon 3:4 KJV).

With that grateful bride I can say, "I have found Him whom my soul loves." Now the earnest desire of my heart is to hold fast to Him, and never again to let Him go. I know of no way to experience unbroken union and communion with our beloved Lord Jesus apart from a conscious, deliberate choice to spend time alone with Him each morning.

MAKING IT PERSONAL

1. Which of the three elements of a quiet time discussed in this chapter (a consistent practice, in the morning, a solitary place) do you find the most difficult?

2. Have you ever had a season when you found yourself taking shortcuts in your devotional life—living in a spiritual fast-food drive-through? Briefly describe the circumstances surrounding that time and some of the consequences you experienced in your walk with God and others.

3. What are the greatest barriers you encounter in maintaining a consistent time alone with the Lord in the morning?

   Ask the Lord what practical steps you could take to overcome those obstacles. Record any insights He gives you.

4. If you have not already established a consistent habit of meeting alone with the Lord, would you purpose in your heart to spend some time in the Word and prayer every morning for the next seven days? Share your commitment with your spouse or a friend and ask that person to help hold you accountable.

FROM THE HEART OF

Vonette Bright

The more time I spend in prayer and devotion, the more I wonder why I do not spend more time! The rewards are far greater than any other way I could spend my time. Time alone with God is how I grow in faith and learn to depend on Christ and walk in Him.

During my daily quiet time, I meet the Lord, listen to Him speak to me from His Word, receive direction for my life, and pour out my heart to Him in prayer. As I spend time with Him, I am renewed, refreshed, and energized in my spirit. This may take a few minutes or several hours. My purpose is to stay before Him until I know I have met with Him.

Start your quiet time with a prayer that God will reveal His truth to you. Practice the presence of God. Picture yourself in His presence and respond accordingly.

Begin your Bible reading with prayer, asking for His insight, direction, and understanding. I suggest reading consecutively through the Bible. You may wish to read a different Bible translation each year (or until you have finished the translation). I have enjoyed the *One Year Bible*, which includes a passage from the Old and New Testaments, as well as a psalm and a proverb.

As you pray, begin with praise and adoration, perhaps using a hymnal. Confess all sin and appropriate God's forgiveness. Talk as you would to your best friend. Divide prayer requests by days of the week to make your list more manageable. Use a prayer journal. Pray through the names of God in Scripture.

Each day, pass on a nugget of truth you received from the Lord that day.

Vonette Bright is a mother of two and grandmother of four. She and her husband, Bill, are co-founders of Campus Crusade for Christ International. For many years, Vonette has been actively involved in launching and providing leadership for national and international prayer movements.

NOTES

PART PAGE: Mrs. Charles E. Cowman, comp., *Streams in the Desert*, vol. 1 (Cowman Publications: 1925; Grand Rapids: Zondervan, c. 1965–66), reading for March 2.

1. Donald S. Whitney, *Spiritual Disciplines for the Christian Life* (Colorado Springs: Navpress, 1991), 88.
2. John Blanchard, *How to Enjoy Your Bible* (Colchester, England: Evangelical, 1984), 104.
3. Larnelle Harris and Phil McHugh, "I Miss My Time with You." Copyright 1980 Lifesong Music/BMI, RIVER OAKS MUSIC/BMI. All rights reserved. Used by permission of Brentwood-Benson Music Publishing, Inc.
4. Horatius Bonar, in *Streams in the Desert*, reading for March 2.
5. Charles H. Spurgeon, *Metropolitan Tabernacle Pulpit* (AGES Software: Albany, Oreg., 1996), 735.
6. Thomas Watson, *Gleanings from Thomas Watson*, comp. Hamilton Smith (Morgan, Pa.: Soli Deo Gloria, 1995), 105–6.
9. Ralph Spaulding Cushman, "The Secret," from *Spiritual Hilltops* (Abingdon-Cokesbury, 1932). Cited in *Masterpieces of Religious Verse*, ed. James Dalton Morrison (Grand Rapids: Baker, 1977), 408–9.
8. *Streams in the Desert*, reading for December 4.

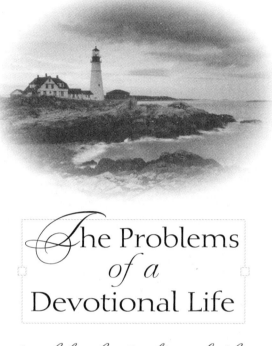

PART FOUR

The Problems of a Devotional Life

I sought him, but I could not find him.

SONG OF SOLOMON 5:6 KJV

I throw myself down in my chamber, and I call in and invite God and His angels thither. And when they are there, I neglect God and His angels for the noise of a fly, for the rattling of a coach, for the whining of a door; I talk on, in the same posture of praying: eyes lifted up, knees bowed down, as though I prayed to God. And if God or His angels should ask me, when I last thought of God in that prayer, I cannot tell.

JOHN DONNE

CHAPTER 6

"The Hard Thing for Me Is..."

Some time ago, I sent a questionnaire to three hundred women from across the United States who had attended one of our ministry's women's conferences. I wanted to hear their hearts in relation to this matter of a daily devotional life. The women were asked to respond to such questions as:

- Why do you believe it is important to have a daily quiet time? (Out of 178 women who returned the questionnaires, 175 indicated they felt it was "very important" to have a consistent, daily quiet time with the Lord.)

- What are some of the benefits you have received from having a regular quiet time?

- What have you found to be the greatest obstacle(s) to a consistent, meaningful devotional life?

- What insights would you like to share with other women about how to have a meaningful devotional life?

I appreciated the thoughtful, candid responses the women

gave to these questions. Many wrote honestly of their struggles and failures in trying to establish a daily quiet time. And many made excellent, practical suggestions that I have found helpful in my own walk.

In this chapter, we will address some of the obstacles these women have encountered in trying to develop a consistent devotional life. (Answers to the questionnaire appear in italics throughout the chapter.) The barriers they identified are ones that most of us have experienced at one time or another in our walk with the Lord. For example, you may have found yourself thinking (or saying) . . .

"I just can't find the time!"

Six years ago, I was single and could focus on the Lord. Now that I have been married for three years and have two small children, it is very difficult for me to find that time. Please help!

By far, this issue of time was the number one obstacle identified by women who responded to our questionnaire.

The fact is, if we don't make a conscious, deliberate effort to set aside time to be with the Lord, other things will demand our attention. One of my spiritual mentors, who is now with the Lord, used to say: "Don't try to squeeze God into an already overcrowded schedule. Determine your schedule around Him!" Several of the women we heard from suggested making an appointment with God and keeping it, as we would any other type of appointment.

Other women commented on the necessity of viewing this time as the most important thing in our lives:

Don't look at prayer and Bible study as something you try to make time for. Look at it as a need—a need that, if not met, could have serious consequences.

Our time with the Lord is the most important part of our day. If we only get that done, we've done the most important activity. If we do not take the time, we've missed the most important and majored on the unimportant. We need to schedule our quiet time or it won't happen.

I have found if I make time, the Lord will give me time for other things.

Puritan pastor William Gurnall (1616–79) considered it unthinkable that a child of God would be unable to find time to read the Book in which God has communicated His love and grace:

> Could God find heart and time to pen and send this love-letter to thee, and thou find none to read and peruse it! The sick man no time to look on his physician's prescription! The condemned malefactor to look on his prince's letter of grace, wherein a pardon is signed![1]

"My life is so busy!"

How do you make life less hectic? Ten- to twelve-hour workdays take their toll. I don't know how to slow down.

Every once in a while, we need to stop and reevaluate our schedule and activities in light of our God-given priorities. This is not easy to do. We tend to think that everything we are doing is essential. While it may be true that everything we are doing is *good,* if we don't have time to cultivate our relationship with the Lord, then undoubtedly we are doing some things that are not on God's agenda for our lives.

If we want to have an intimate relationship with the Lord Jesus, we must be willing to bring all our activities under the scrutiny of His Spirit and to let Him show us which ones are not His priorities for us—at least for that season of our lives. (Your husband or another mature believer may be a great asset in helping you think through those activities.)

If you are a parent, you may also find it necessary to evaluate the activities that your children are involved in. I have observed many well-meaning parents who live breathless, out-of-control lives because their children are enrolled in every available extracurricular program—sports, private music lessons, band, choir, drama—in addition to being encouraged (or permitted) to be involved in a variety of hobbies and recreation, a constant whirlwind of social activities, and every youth group function. Those parents seem to spend their lives running around with their children from one function to the next. Not only does this keep them on the go from early in the morning till late at night, but it can also create in their children an "activity addiction" that decreases their children's ability to have a quiet heart and curbs their appetite for the Word of God and prayer.

Whether our own activities or those of our children, all must be evaluated in light of our ultimate, eternal priorities. One of the women we surveyed expressed this point particularly well:

> It is worth it to put all else aside for a quiet time with God. The laundry will wait. Time with the Lord is of eternal value. In the light of eternity, what difference will all these things make?

The powerful seventeenth-century preacher Lewis Bayly urged his hearers to make choices in this life that they would be glad to have made in eternity:

> But it may be thou wilt say, that thy business will not permit thee so much time, as to read every morning a chapter. O man, remember that thy life is but short, and that all this business is but for the use of this short life; but salvation or damnation is everlasting! Rise up, therefore, every morning by so much time the earlier: defraud thy foggy flesh of so much sleep; but rob not thy soul of her food, nor God of His service; and serve the Almighty duly whilst thou hast time and health.[2]

"I just can't fit everything into my day."

It's hard to be consistent in my quiet time when I work until four or five, come home, cook, clean, and by that time I'm exhausted. Then I have a responsibility of pleasing my husband. Sometimes I feel guilty, thinking, "Why can't I get it all together and be more organized?"

As we evaluate our schedules in light of our God-given priorities, we must then determine to eliminate (or limit) any activities that hinder us from fulfilling those priorities.

Some of these decisions are more clear-cut than others. For example, one of the difficult, but obvious, decisions I have had to make in recent years is to turn off the television. I live alone and found myself at one point turning the television on when I got home at night, just for the noise and companionship. Precious hours were being expended on mindless activity—hours that might have been used to nurture my spirit or to minister to the needs of others. Then I wondered why I couldn't find enough time to spend alone with the Lord.

In my heart, I knew my spiritual life would be better off if I didn't have the TV on. Finally, I waved the "white flag of surrender," said, "Yes, Lord," and made a commitment to not watch television anytime that I am alone.

That decision has proved to be one of the best I have ever made. Not only do I have more time to devote to my relationship with the Lord, but I also have a greater appetite for spiritual things because I am not feasting on the things of this world.

I have had to say no to other types of activities, as well—some of them wholesome, but none of them as important as sitting at the feet of Jesus and listening to His Word. Here's what some of the women we surveyed had to say about selecting our activities in light of our priorities:

We women make time to shop! We must make time for God.

Do not waste time on soaps, shopping, etc. Make time to spend with the Lord daily—nothing is more important.

Guard against overcommitment. Weigh very carefully new undertakings. Will it take time away from the feet of Jesus and put me in another kitchen?

As tough as it may be to admit, if you and I are too busy to cultivate our relationship with God, then something is wrong—something has to change. The change required may be a relatively minor adjustment in our schedule, or it may be a drastic reordering of priorities.

Many of the women who responded to our survey indicated that they just can't juggle the demands of a full-time job, rearing children, meeting the needs of a husband, and keeping up a home and have any quality time left to spend with the Lord. The Scripture clearly teaches that a wife and mother is to devote her attention to the needs of her husband, children, and home (Titus 2:4–5). But is it possible that the additional responsibility of working outside the home is keeping some women from devoting themselves to the "one thing [that] is needed" (Luke 10:42)?

There are many factors that go into a woman's deciding to have a job outside the home; but I believe Christian women must be encouraged to make that decision in light of the things that matter most in this life and for all eternity. The point is, if you cannot have a job *and* manage your household *and* find time to get to know God, then ask God to show you (and your husband) how you can be released to come back into your home so you can focus on becoming a woman who knows and walks with God.

One woman who responded to our questionnaire put it this way:

Choose to do it! Life is choices. We make daily choices in so many areas of our lives. Do we really believe that meeting with God is as important and necessary as our daily physical food? Then choose to make it a priority!

"My time with the Lord often seems hurried."

In the morning, I am rushed; in the evening, I am tired and can't concentrate.

I have come to believe that a rushed or hurried attitude is one of the deadliest enemies of an effective devotional life. Some time ago, I was exercising on the treadmill while listening to a tape on which my friend, Dr. Henry Blackaby (the author of *Experiencing God*), was being interviewed about his personal devotional life. Dr. Blackaby said something in that interview that has profoundly impacted my own time with the Lord.

He told of a time in the past when he had found himself getting up each morning to meet with the Lord, but having to rush that time in order to attend to the various responsibilities of the day. He shared how God had convicted him that it was a grievous offense to "hurry the God of the universe," and how he determined to move his quiet time up a half hour earlier so he would not be rushed. He did so but found that he still ended up being hurried, so he moved the time up another half hour earlier. Dr. Blackaby said, "I kept moving the time up in the morning, until I knew that I could meet with God as long as He wanted to meet with me, without being hurried."

As I heard those words from a busy man who evidences a deep, steady, fruitful walk with God, I purposed in my heart to do whatever was necessary to secure unhurried time to let God speak to me on a daily basis. I have had to make adjustments in my schedule; I have had to make some "sacrifices." But the fruit of spending unhurried time with Him has been precious and sweet.

As great a man of God as Martyn Lloyd-Jones had to fight the tendency to hurry God:

One day recently I wanted to thank God in a certain matter; but at the time I also had business in hand which needed urgent attention. I was on the point of offering up a hurried word of thanksgiving to God in order that I might return to the urgent task; but realizing what was happening, I suddenly said to myself: "That is not the way to thank God. Do you realize whom you are about to thank?" Everything must be laid aside when you are turning to Him; everything, everyone, all things, however urgent. What are they compared to Him? Stop! Pause! Wait! Recollect! Realize what you are doing.[3]

"How do I deal with interruptions and distractions?"

I sit down with my Bible, read a sentence, the phone rings, the dryer goes off, the TV my husband is watching is too loud . . .

I happen to be an easily distracted person. In fact, in the last few hours since I began working on this chapter, I have fought a steady stream of distractions: a loud utility truck pulled up on the street outside my window and sat there for some thirty minutes—I had to get up and go close the window so I could concentrate; I got thirsty and had to go upstairs to get something to drink; I got cold and had to go upstairs and put on warmer clothes; I stopped to check my E-mail messages, which led to checking my voice mail messages, which led to taking care of several items of business that had nothing to do with this book; I got up to get rid of a spider that I noticed climbing up the wall; finally, I was so tired I had to lie down for a brief nap! (As I was writing this paragraph, I managed to create yet another distraction by pulling the power cord on my computer and losing everything I had written in the last fifteen minutes.)

All of these distractions took place when no one else was in the house. When you add in hungry or cranky children, barking dogs, telephone calls, and repairmen at the door, it can be extremely difficult to concentrate on Bible reading and prayer.

There will always be possible distractions, but the following insights have been helpful to me.

Many distractions can be avoided simply by getting up earlier. We have seen that it was Jesus' practice to get up before daybreak so that He might enjoy unhurried communion with His Father before the crowds began to press in on Him. As I have already mentioned, once the phone calls begin to come into my office at home, I know it is going to be much more difficult for me to get a quiet heart before the Lord.

Ask God to help you recognize and ignore unnecessary distractions. For example, I have had to learn that I don't have to jump to answer the phone every time it rings.

Years ago, I had the honor of meeting with President Ronald Reagan. Out of respect for the man and his position, I would not have considered taking a phone call during that meeting. When I am in staff meetings or counseling sessions, I generally ask my staff to hold all phone calls except for emergencies. Yet how often have I found myself in the middle of an appointment with the King of the universe, jumping up to answer every phone call as if it were more important than He! Is it not disrespectful for me to put God "on hold" while I stop to attend to every detail that comes my way?

Be flexible in responding to "divine interruptions." Have you ever found yourself in the middle of reading the Word or praying, only to respond in anger or impatience to a child, a mate, or a friend who interrupts you with a genuine need?

Even Jesus had His quiet time interrupted. In the passage we have already examined in Mark 1, Jesus was interrupted by His disciples coming and telling Him, "Everyone is looking for you!" (v. 37). Because He had a listening ear, Jesus was tuned to the will of His Father and able to discern when an interruption was God-sent. In this case, Jesus realized it was time to go and preach in the nearby villages. Because He was sensitive to the Father, He could respond to interruptions without becoming irritable.

"When I try to read or pray, my mind wanders. I can't concentrate."

When it comes to my own quiet time, many of the distractions are not external, but internal. I no sooner sit down in my "quiet time chair" than I begin thinking of a whole host of things I need to do—thank-you notes to be written, calls to be made, tasks to be completed at work . . . I may even get a sudden, new burden for housecleaning!

The seventeenth-century English poet John Donne expressed this tendency so familiar to anyone who has ever sought to set his heart on things above:

> A memory of yesterday's pleasures, a fear of tomorrow's dangers, a straw under my knee, a noise in my ear, a light in mine eye, an anything, a nothing, a fancy, a chimera in my brain, troubles me in my prayer.[4]

I have found that it often takes time to get a quiet heart before the Lord. You may want to start your time with the Lord by singing some worshipful choruses, reading aloud a psalm of praise, and asking the Lord to settle your heart in His presence. When I am struggling to concentrate, I will sometimes stop and ask the Lord to help me "take captive every thought to make it obedient to Christ" (2 Corinthians 10:5).

When unrelated thoughts or tasks come to mind, rather than stopping to attend to them at the moment or trying to remember them until later, simply jot them down on a notepad. In fact, rather than fighting those thoughts, as you write them down they can become direction for specific prayer. I find that as I place those concerns before the Lord, He gives me wisdom and insight I need to deal with those matters, as well as helping me to prioritize my day.

Some of the woman we surveyed shared that praying while they were out walking helped them to stay focused on the Lord. Reading Scripture aloud, praying aloud, writing down insights from the Word, and writing your prayers are other practices that can help increase concentration.

"What if I have young children?"

How do you maintain a quality devotional life when you have younger children whose radar goes off the minute you get out of bed?

Recently, I asked a number of older, godly women how they were able to have consistent devotions when their children were young. Some admitted that they didn't; most acknowledged that it was not easy; but they all agreed that it must be a priority. Here are some practical ideas they shared.

Take time when they are asleep. Ask God to awaken you in the middle of the night or when you have had enough sleep. Many times I had my quiet time with my children beside me, or while I was nursing an infant.

(A mother of eight) *Once my kids are up does not work for me; however, between midnight and 3:00 A.M. usually is possible. I believe moms may have to yield their right to a picture-perfect quiet time and realize they can meet the Lord even while they meet physical and emotional needs for their family. Sometimes, when I have read only a few verses, but I have been obedient that day with my time, and my heart attitudes have honored Christ, I am more content than when I dutifully "check off" my quiet time, but have spent the day in my own abilities, resentful of the demands on my time.*

The only way I've been able to have consistent devotions with small children is to get up before they do. This season of life does not always lend itself to longer, in-depth study of the Word, but even a few verses and a short prayer and worship time have helped me through many days. God understands our circumstances and our heart's desire to meet with Him. We can't put ourselves on a guilt trip at this stage of life when we can't spend as much time as we'd like in the Word. But it must still be our top priority, however brief it may be.

Ask God to protect those times. Children should be instructed that this is a priority and to leave Mom alone unless there is an emergency. They can and do learn. I got up earlier than they got up. I spent time with God during their naps. Later, I spent time with God right after they left for school.

When our daughter was two to three years old, we had a clock which gave the time every thirty minutes. I would tell Renee that I was having time with Jesus. She would sit with her book (upside down sometimes) and have her quiet time. After the bird cuckooed the next thirty minutes, we would have time as mom and daughter. She knew to let me have that time between cuckoos!

You have to be determined and creative. I remember many times during those early years rocking a sick child in my arms and bouncing another on my feet and turning on the Bible on cassette, and praying, "Lord, give me something to encourage my soul to faith." As the Lord would speak to me, I would write it down and write a prayer back to Him and simply say, "Lord, make it so in my life."

Remember that this season will not last forever. It is so important to maintain our personal time with the Lord during these years. However, the time and place may vary. We must find it when and where we can. God loves us and understands our needs. He will faithfully meet us as we faithfully seek His face. When my children were small, I posted verses on cabinets and over the sink, even on the dash of the car. This made memorization and meditation of Scripture so much easier. If we see them and think on them long enough, those verses will soon become a part of our lives.

It may not be easy, but if you really, really want to meet with God, you will find a way to do it!

I am told that Susannah Wesley, mother of nineteen children (nine of whom died in infancy), managed to spend an hour in the morning, an hour in the evening, and often an hour at noon alone with the Lord. Her children learned early that time alone with God was a sacred necessity. Little wonder, then, that two of her sons, John and Charles, grew up to become mighty servants in the kingdom of Christ.

"I'm so exhausted that I don't have the energy to have a quiet time."

As a single parent, I have so little energy. My day starts early, and by the end of the day, I am fatigued. I often have to stop my devotional reading because my eyes won't stay open and I don't know what I've just read.

Jesus' disciples knew all about being too tired to pray. At the moment that their dearest Friend needed them to keep spiritual watch with Him, emotionally and physically exhausted, they succumbed to sleep. Jesus did not berate them. But He did remind them that the failure to "watch and pray" would leave them vulnerable to temptation.

I have discovered that the more tired I am, the more I need the refreshing of His presence. Yes, there are those days when the eyelids are heavy. But there is something energizing about time spent in the Word, praise, and prayer. Perhaps that is because when we express our weakness and need to God, He pours out His grace.

Look for creative ways to wake up and stay awake: get out of bed (for me, staying in bed is a sure way to fall asleep); take a shower; stand or walk to pray; sing; weather permitting, have your quiet time outside.

If you are consistently exhausted, ask yourself, "Why am I tired?" Is there a simple physical explanation that would be helped by the right combination of vitamins, diet, and exercise? (Exercise is close to the top of my "least favorite things to do" list. But I do it regularly, because it gives me greater physical stamina and strength to seek the Lord and to fulfill the responsibilities He has entrusted to me.) Are you making unwise choices with your schedule that are contributing to your weariness? Are you doing some things that aren't on God's agenda for your life at this season?

It may be that you are in a season of life that is unusually draining—during a pregnancy, after the birth of a child, following major surgery, or while caring for a parent with a terminal illness. If so, don't let the Enemy convince you that your tiredness is a spiritual problem; and don't let him use your tiredness as an excuse for not seeking the Lord.

One day a young mother sought me out for counsel. She had just had her fourth child and was disturbed that she had no desire for the Word or prayer. She felt guilty and was even wondering if perhaps she was not a Christian at all. Of course, only the Holy Spirit could give her assurance of salvation, but as I listened, I sensed that physical exhaustion due to nursing an infant and inadequate sleep probably accounted for most of what she was experiencing.

Rather than put her on a further guilt trip, I shared with her one of my favorite Old Testament names for God: El Shaddai. Our English Bibles translate that Hebrew name as "Almighty God" or the "All-Sufficient One." But the root word for El Shaddai is the word *shad*, the Hebrew word for "breast." This name pictures God as the "breasted One." Much as a nursing mother pours herself out to satisfy the thirst of her infant, causing the fretful child to be calmed at the mother's breast, so El Shaddai "pours Himself into believing lives"[5] and satisfies His children's thirsty, fretful hearts.

I encouraged that frazzled young mother to meditate on El Shaddai, even as she nursed her own infant in the night hours, and to allow the Lord to satisfy and fill her with His unconditional love. As we prayed together, I asked God to hold this fragile woman close to Himself and to pour Himself into her life. At that moment, she began to cry—tears of release—as the Holy Spirit ministered grace to her heart and she surrendered herself to the tender love of El Shaddai.

When your body is weary, ask God for the physical strength necessary to do His will; He knows your needs and can be trusted to meet them. In Jesus' time of greatest need, as He prayed in the Garden of Gethsemane, Luke's account tells us that "an angel from heaven appeared to him and strengthened him" (Luke 22:43). As you pray, exercise faith in His promise:

*He giveth power to the faint; and to them that have no might he in-
creaseth strength. Even the youths shall faint and be weary, and the
young men shall utterly fall: but they that wait upon the LORD shall renew their strength; they shall mount up with wings as eagles; they shall
run, and not be weary; and they shall walk, and not faint.* (ISAIAH
40:29–31 KJV)

"My husband isn't supportive."

*How can I deal with a husband who says he is a Christian, yet discour-
ages me from having my quiet time? I try to have it when he is not at
home. Then he asks why I don't get much done around the house after I
get home from work. He almost seems jealous of my time with the Lord.
He does not read his Bible or spend time in prayer on his own.*

Other women we surveyed indicated that they struggle
with having a non-Christian husband who resists their in-
volvement with the Lord.

The wise woman will look for ways to prioritize both her
relationship with the Lord and with her husband. If your husband is jealous of the time you are spending with the Lord, ask
Him to show you what is at the heart of his frustration. Ask
yourself such questions as:

- Does my husband feel that he is not really important to
  me? Have I made him feel that he has to compete with
  God for my time and attention?
- Does my husband or family have physical or practical
  needs that I have not been meeting?
- Do I make myself available to my husband—to spend
  time with him, to listen to him?
- Do I express genuine interest in the things that are im-
  portant to him?
- Am I being sensitive to the best time to meet with the
  Lord?
- Am I using my quiet time as an excuse for neglecting oth-

er responsibilities in my home?

- Does my husband feel that I look down on him as being "unspiritual"? Have I been critical of him because of his lack of interest in spiritual things? Have I communicated a spiritual "superiority complex"?

In most cases, a wife's duties to her husband and her love for the Lord should not be in conflict, for both are the will of God. The time a woman spends in the Word and prayer should not keep her from meeting the needs of her husband and children—to the contrary, it should make her a *better* wife and mother. As she spends time with the Lord, she will be more reverent, loving, kind, and attentive toward her husband; she will have a grateful, humble, joyous spirit; and she will seek to be faithful in meeting the practical needs of her household.

"Sometimes I feel like I'm having my quiet time just out of duty."

> *My quiet time seems to have become legalistic—something to check off my "to do" list each day. I feel if I really loved the Lord I would jump out of bed and run to spend time with Him.*

First of all, our feelings are rarely a reliable gauge of reality. Further, there is value in maintaining any good habit, even when it is not motivated by warm feelings or intense desire. Frequently, the faithful carrying out of a discipline will result in greater desire. For example, a woman may find it difficult to honor her parents or her husband because she does not *feel* warm, loving thoughts toward them. But if she will choose to honor them and to *act* in a loving way, regardless of how she feels, she may well find that the feelings follow.

So it is in our walk with the Lord. We cannot depend on our feelings. But our heart's devotion for Him will deepen and grow as we choose to put Him first and invest time in that relationship, regardless of how we feel.

Several of the women we surveyed commented on how God blesses when we make right choices:

Sometimes, when we just do it out of obedience, then our hearts are drawn to Him in devotion.

Even when it feels like a duty, even when I seem to be just going through the motions, even when it doesn't feel meaningful, God's blessings come from the quiet times.

I've been praying daily for three years. It started out of duty and I just followed the "steps." But now that our relationship has been established, my quiet times are definitely out of devotion.

C. H. Spurgeon encouraged people to pray whether or not they felt like it:

We should pray when we are in a praying mood, for it would be sinful to neglect so fair an opportunity. We should pray when we are not in the proper mood, for it would be dangerous to remain in so unhealthy a condition.[6]

"How do you handle dry spells?"

What has happened when the Bible becomes dry and boring—especially when it used to be so wonderful? Why did I lose my desire?

Psalms 42 and 43 read like the journal of a believer in the throes of a spiritual dry spell. The psalmist cries out,

> *My soul thirsts for God, for the living God.*
> *When can I go and meet with God?. . .*
> *Why are you downcast, O my soul?*
> *Why so disturbed within me?*

—PSALM 42:2, 5

In the midst of this spiritual desert, he first looks back and remembers the joy he has experienced in God's presence in the past:

> *These things I remember*
> > *as I pour out my soul:*
> *how I used to go with the multitude,*
> > *leading the procession to the house of God,*
> *with shouts of joy and thanksgiving.*
>
> —PSALM 42:4

By faith, he also looks ahead to the day when the joy will be restored:

> *Put your hope in God,*
> > *for I will yet praise him,*
> > *my Savior and my God.*
>
> —PSALM 42:5–6

In the meantime, he determines to look up:

> *My soul is downcast within me;*
> > *therefore I will remember you. . . .*
> *By day the* LORD *directs his love,*
> > *at night his song is with me—*
> > *a prayer to the God of my life.*
>
> —PSALM 42:6, 8

During seasons of spiritual dryness, ask God to show you any specific issues that may be creating a barrier in your relationship with Him. Is there any known sin that you have not confessed or repented of? Is there unforgiveness in your heart toward a family member or an individual who has wronged you? Is there some step of obedience you know God wants you to take that you have delayed? Some of the women we surveyed spoke of allowing anger or disappointment to put up walls in their relationship with God. All of these issues can produce spiritual dryness.

Sometimes spiritual dry spells are simply God's way of revealing what is in our heart—whether we love Him because of the spiritual sensations He gives us, or whether we love Him just because He is God.

At other times, dry spells are an evidence that we are in a rut in our devotional life. We may have become too focused on the mechanics of what we are doing, rather than the meaning. Many times this can be dealt with by varying our routine. Recently when I felt the need for freshness in my devotional life, I took a few days out from my normal Bible reading schedule to review and meditate on some passages that I had memorized earlier.

One of the women who responded to our survey shared how important it is to stay committed to a relationship, even through the tough times:

> I love my husband of thirty-eight years, [and] we were determined to get through the tough times together. Quitting and losing out on the benefits would have been the easy way. I am determined to love and obey the Lord with all my heart. At times, it would be easy to quit, but, oh, the benefits I would lose. I know that we will get through the tough times together!

"Truthfully, I don't have a strong desire to spend time with God."

> What I need is a fresh touch from God to give me the desire to be in the Word more.

We have all faced times when we just didn't have the hunger or desire to meet with the Lord. In the physical realm, when we are hungry, we eat, at which point we are no longer hungry. The more we eat, the less hungry we are. However, in the spiritual world, just the opposite is true. The more we eat spiritual food, the more hungry we become and the more we want to eat. The more you taste of the Word of God, the more you will long for it. The more you partake of Jesus, the Bread of Life, the more you will hunger for Him. If you do not have an appetite for spiritual food, there is a good chance you have not been fueling that appetite.

A closely related reason for lack of spiritual desire is that we may be filling ourselves with what the world has to offer, leaving us with little appetite for spiritual food. When you tell your children they can't eat candy at five o'clock in the afternoon "because it will spoil your appetite," you realize that if they get filled with the quick rush that sugar provides, they will not be hungry for the food you know they really need.

When the children of Israel moved from Egypt into the wilderness of Sinai, it took them a while to acquire an appetite for manna, which seemed bland and boring compared to the spice and variety of the "onions, leeks, and garlic" they had enjoyed in Egypt. But God was interested in more than satisfying their taste buds; He knew what would really nourish and sustain them for the years in the wilderness. He wanted to wean them from the short-lived, cheap thrills of Egypt so He could introduce them to the true joys of being fed by His hand and so He could cultivate in them a longing for the Promised Land.

If you are in the habit of feasting on what the world has to offer—books, magazines, radio, music, television, videos, newspapers, catalogues, shopping malls—you probably have little appetite for the Word and prayer.

Do you want to increase your hunger for the Lord? Try weaning yourself from the world's diet—be prepared for some withdrawal symptoms when you turn off the radio and the TV and eliminate unnecessary activities. Then begin feeding on the Word of God. At first, it may seem bland and boring; but, in time, you will discover that it satisfies in a far deeper, richer way than those things you once thought were so filling.

"Sometimes God seems a million miles away."

I seem to be having a daily monologue.

There are times when God withholds from us the conscious sense of His presence—times that God seems far away and we no longer have feelings of intimacy we may once have enjoyed. I believe this is because He wants us to learn to walk by faith and to seek Him with all our hearts.

In the midst of extreme suffering, Job struggled to believe that God was there when he could not sense His presence.

> *Behold, I go forward, but he is not there; and backward, but I cannot perceive him: on the left hand, where he doth work, but I cannot behold him: he hideth himself on the right hand, that I cannot see him.* (JOB 23:8–9 KJV)

Then, with eyes of faith, Job declared what he knew to be true and affirmed his commitment to cling to the Lord and His Word, in spite of what his feelings told him:

> *But he knoweth the way that I take: when he hath tried me, I shall come forth as gold. . . . Neither have I gone back from the commandment of his lips; I have esteemed the words of his mouth more than my necessary food.* (JOB 23:10, 12 KJV)

The Song of Solomon records two seasons in which the Shulammite bride had a similar experience: "By night on my bed I sought him whom my soul loveth: I sought him, but I found him not. . . . My beloved had withdrawn himself, and was gone" (3:1; 5:6 KJV). In both instances, the painful (though only perceived) absence caused the troubled bride to pursue her Beloved earnestly until she found him. Her diligent search was rewarded with a restored consciousness of His presence, as well as a renewed determination to stay close by His side. When she finally found her Beloved, she said, "I held him, and would not let him go" (3:4).

Younger, less mature believers are often granted a special, conscious sense of God's presence. As we grow, He provides opportunities for us to trust Him when we cannot see Him. God is pleased with the faith that is strengthened in the darkness. That is what is at the heart of Isaiah's exhortation to those who have faithfully followed the Lord but cannot sense His presence:

> Who among you fears the LORD
>   and obeys the word of his servant?
> Let him who walks in the dark,
>   who has no light,
> trust in the name of the LORD
>   and rely on his God.
>
> —ISAIAH 50:10

The Enemy will throw these and other obstacles in our path to try to get us to live the Christian life apart from consistent, daily time in God's presence. At times you will get discouraged and may feel like throwing in the towel. Don't quit! Keep pursuing Him. Your search will be rewarded.

Making It Personal

1. Which of the obstacles discussed in this chapter do you most identify with? What suggestions would you make to a friend who was struggling with the same obstacles?

2. Think through your current schedule and identify any activities that may be hindering you from adequately prioritizing your relationship with the Lord.

3. What steps do you need to take to ensure that your relationship with the Lord is the most important priority in your life? Share those steps with a friend who will help hold you accountable.

4. Whom do you know who has a consistent devotional life? Ask one or more of those individuals to share with you how they have dealt with the specific obstacles you have encountered.

FROM THE HEART OF
Barbara Rainey

As a new believer, I learned about the importance of a daily quiet time. (I was a nineteen-year-old sophomore in college.) I began a prayer journal and some Bible reading and was fairly consistent through college and into my early years of marriage. In fact, one of my adjustments in marriage was discovering that my husband did not have the same kind of structured daily quiet time that I did.

This became a source of spiritual pride in my life. I thought I was more spiritually mature than he because of my discipline. The truth is, my relationship with God was more legalistic, while my husband's was more personal and real.

As our children were born and my responsibilities as a mom increased, my spiritual disciplines were affected. I would get into a routine, only to have it fall apart within a few weeks. I struggled with the whole issue for years, wanting to do what was right, wanting to grow, but feeling like a failure much of the time.

I finally came to the place where I decided to quit trying. It wasn't a decision to quit growing, but to stop expecting myself to fit my mental picture of what a "spiritual Christian" should look like. I still prayed every day, but I didn't sit down with a list for a certain amount of time.

While I feel I needed to go through that process, I do believe I wasn't in the Word enough and didn't pray as purposefully as I might have and, consequently, may have missed some of what God intended for me during those years.

Now I am in a different season of life, with four children married or in college and a little more control over my time. Presently I am reading through the Bible in a year—I'm already almost a month behind, but I find the structure is necessary for me, even if it takes two years instead of one.

I do believe that connecting with the Lord on a daily basis is essential. Yes, it is something we do to seek Him, but it is the Holy Spirit who leads and enables us to become like Him.

Barbara Rainey is the mother of six children. Her husband, Dennis, is the executive director and cofounder of FamilyLife (a division of Campus Crusade for Christ). Barbara and Dennis have coauthored five books on marriage and family relationships, and have spoken together at FamilyLife Conferences throughout North America and abroad.

NOTES

PART PAGE: From a sermon preached at the funeral of Sir William Cokayne. Cited in *The English Spirit: The Little Gidding Anthology of English Spirituality* (Nashville: Abingdon, 1987), 79.

1. William Gurnall, *Gleanings from William Gurnall*, comp. Hamilton Smith (Morgan, Pa.: Soli Deo Gloria, 1996), 104–5.

2. Lewis Bayly, *The Practice of Piety* (1862; reprint, Morgan, Pa.: Soli Deo Gloria, 1995), 107.

3. D. M. Lloyd-Jones, *God's Ultimate Purpose: An Exposition of Ephesians 1:1 to 23* (Grand Rapids: Baker, 1986), 330.

4. From a sermon preached at the funeral of Sir William Cokayne. Cited in *The English Spirit*, 79.

5. *The Scofield Reference Bible* (New York: Oxford Univ. Press, 1945), 26. Note on Genesis 17:1.

6. Charles H. Spurgeon, *Metropolitan Tabernacle Pulpit* (AGES Software: Albany, Oreg., 1996), 71.

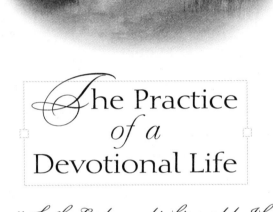

PART FIVE

The Practice
of a
Devotional Life

I wait for the Lord . . . and in his word do I hope.
PSALM 130:5 KJV

Every morning, day in and day out, I get alone with God. I would not dream of going to my office before first of all spending time alone with Him. Nor would I attempt to carry on my church work without first meeting God, morning by morning. Directly after breakfast I retire to my study, close the door, and there spend the first hour alone with God. For over fifty years now I have observed the Morning Watch. If God has used me in any way down through the years it is because I have met Him morning by morning. I solve my problems before I come to them. Without the Morning Watch my work would be ineffective. I would be weak and helpless. It is only when I wait upon Him that I become strong spiritually.

OSWALD J. SMITH

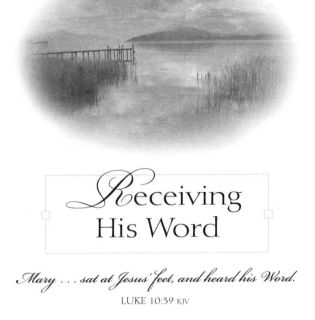

Receiving His Word

Mary . . . sat at Jesus' feet, and heard his Word.

LUKE 10:39 KJV

I saw that the most important thing was to give myself to the reading of the Word of God, and to meditation on it, that thus my heart might be comforted, encouraged, warned, reproved, instructed; and that thus, by means of the Word of God, whilst meditating on it, my heart might be brought into experimental communion with the Lord.

I began therefore to meditate on the New Testament from the beginning, early in the morning. The first thing I did, after having asked in a few words the Lord's blessing upon His precious Word, was to begin to meditate on the Word of God, searching as it were into every verse to get blessing out of it.

GEORGE MÜLLER

CHAPTER 7

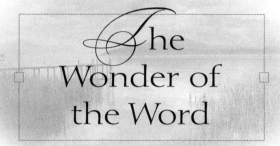

The Wonder of the Word

"I must have a Bible of my own! I must have one, if I have to save up for it for ten years!"

The year was 1794. For as long as she could remember, little Mary Jones had yearned to hold a Bible in her hands so that she might read it for herself. For years, she had sat at night on her weaver father's lap and listened to him tell stories of Abraham, Joseph, David, and Daniel. But her family was far too poor to afford a Bible, even if one had been available, for Bibles could scarcely be found in all of Wales during those days.

Two years earlier, Mrs. Evans, the wife of a nearby farmer, having learned of Mary's longing to read the Bible, had promised the child that when she learned to read, she could come to their house and read their Bible. As soon as the first school opened in a neighboring village, Mary had eagerly set about learning to read.

Now, the ten-year-old girl had just walked two miles from the North Wales village of Llanfihangel to the Evanses' farm. The distance was no object to the eager child: "I'd walk farther than that for such a pleasure, ma'am!" she said to Mrs. Evans.

When once Mary finally was left alone in the room with the Bible, she reverently lifted off the white napkin that covered and protected the cherished Book. Then, with trembling hands, she opened the Book to the fifth chapter of John where her eyes lit on the words, "Search the scriptures; for in them ye think ye have eternal life: and they are they which testify of me" (John 5:39 KJV). Confident that God had spoken to her directly, she earnestly vowed to search His Word with all her heart.

Every Saturday from that point on she made the journey to the Evanses' farm, where she read, studied, and memorized entire chapters from the borrowed Bible. All the time, however, her heart ached, so great was her yearning to have a Bible of her own. She purposed that she must have a Bible, at any cost.

For the next six years, in addition to her studies at school and the many chores to be tended to at home, Mary used every available moment to do odd jobs for friends and neighbors. Every penny she earned was carefully laid aside, until at long last she had saved enough to buy a Bible of her own.

When she learned that the closest place a Bible could be purchased was the town of Bala, some twenty-five miles away, there was no question in her mind about what she must do. With hope in her heart, she started out early one morning, walking barefoot so as not to ruin her one pair of shoes. Before she reached her destination, her feet were blistered and cut from the stones in the road.

Physically weary, but barely able to contain her excitement that her lifelong goal should be so nearly realized, Mary finally arrived in Bala, where she poured out her story to the minister, Mr. Charles. When she had finished, Mr. Charles reluctantly informed her that the last of the Bibles available for purchase had already been sold and that the handful of remaining Bibles had been promised to others. Furthermore, the Society that had printed the small quantity of Welsh Bibles did not intend to print any more.

So great was Mary's disappointment that she began to sob

uncontrollably. Touched by the intensity of her passion to have a Bible of her own, Mr. Charles decided that she must have one of the few Bibles left in his possession. Words cannot describe the ecstasy Mary felt as Mr. Charles placed into her hands the precious treasure for which she had prayed, wept, and hoarded all these years. Her heart sang as she walked the twenty-five miles back home, carrying her very own Bible, the Book that would remain her dearest friend and companion throughout her life.[1]

If God Had Never Spoken

Have you ever thought about what life would be like if God had never spoken? What if He had never communicated with man? What if He had never given us His written Word? Try to imagine a world in which no one had ever heard the voice of God, a world in which there was no Bible.

We would know there *is* a God, because "the heavens declare the glory of God" (Psalm 19:1). But how would we know what He is like? We were created to bring Him pleasure (Revelation 4:11 KJV). But how would we know what pleases Him?

Had God not chosen to speak, to reveal Himself, we would have no standard for right and wrong. We would not know how we are to live. We might experience some vague sense of guilt when we sinned, but we would not know why; nor would we know what to do about our sin. We would have no way of communicating with our Creator. Our lives would be pointless and frustrating.

Imagine having to go through life without knowing anything of the promises of God, the commands of God, the love and mercy of God, the will of God, or the ways of God.

Thankfully, we do not have to exist in such a spiritual vacuum. God *has* spoken. He *has* revealed Himself to man. Have you ever stopped to consider what that really means?

There are many natural wonders on our planet. And man has engineered, designed, and produced many scientific and technological marvels. But none comes close to equaling the wonder of those three small words found in the first chapter of Genesis: *"And God said . . ."*

Think of it! The eternal God and Creator of the universe, the One who holds all the bodies of water on the earth in the palm of His hand, the One who uses the continents as His footstool, the One who measures the span of the universe with the width of His hand—that God has spoken to *us*, His finite but infinitely loved creatures.

In the spiritual realm, God has given us many marvelous gifts—divine wonders that make us stand in awe of His greatness, His power, and His love. The creation of the world, the Incarnation of the Lord Jesus, the miracle of the new birth—each of these marvels is inextricably linked to the *Word of God*.

When God *said*, "Let there be light," there *was* light. The "mere" spoken Word of God brought into being our entire universe. The apostle Peter reminds us that "by God's word the heavens existed and the earth was formed" (2 Peter 3:5).

God's Word was active, not only in Creation, but also in the Incarnation. When the Lord of glory came to this earth as an infant in Bethlehem, *God* was speaking. "The Word became flesh and made his dwelling among us" (John 1:14).

It is that same Word, planted by the Spirit of God in our hearts, that causes us to be born again: "For you have been born again, not of perishable seed, but of imperishable, through the living and enduring word of God" (1 Peter 1:23).

DELIGHTING IN HIS WORD

The older I get and the more I delve into the riches of God's Word, the more I find myself cherishing it, standing in awe of it, and delighting in it "like one who finds great spoil" (Psalm 119:162). I think this is what the psalmist must have felt as he contemplated the portion of God's Word that existed in his day. Throughout Psalm 119, King David seems hardly able to find adequate words to describe what he feels about the Word of God:

Thy testimonies also are my delight and my counsellors. . . .
O how I love thy law! It is my meditation all the day. . . .
How sweet are thy words unto my taste! yea, sweeter than
*   honey to my mouth! . . .*
I love thy commandments above gold; yea, above fine gold. .
.

Thy word is very pure: therefore thy servant loveth it. . . .
My heart standeth in awe of thy word.

—PSALM 119:24, 97, 103, 127, 140, 161 KJV

David was not the only one to feel this way. No other book in history has received the acclaim and adulation given to the Bible. Listen to what some renowned men and women have said about the Bible:

The Bible is a book in comparison with which all others in my eyes are of minor importance; and which in all my perplexities and distresses has never failed to give me light and strength. (ROBERT E. LEE)

This great book . . . is the best gift God has given to man. (ABRAHAM LINCOLN)

The books of men have their day and grow obsolete. God's Word is like Himself, "the same yesterday, today, and forever." (ROBERT PAYNE SMITH)

After more than sixty years of almost daily reading of the Bible, I never fail to find it always new and marvelously in tune with the changing needs of every day. (CECIL B. DEMILLE)

To what greater inspiration and counsel can we turn than to the imperishable truth to be found in this treasure house, the Bible? (QUEEN ELIZABETH II)

The highest earthly enjoyments are but a shadow of the joy I find in reading God's Word. (LADY JANE GREY)

The Bible is the greatest benefit which the human race has ever experienced. . . . A single line in the Bible has consoled me more than all the books I read beside. (IMMANUEL KANT)

The Bible is God's chart for you to steer by, to keep you from the bottom of the sea, and to show you where the harbor is, and how to reach it without running on rocks and bars. (HENRY WARD BEECHER)

I hold one single sentence out of God's Word to be of more certainty and of more power than all the discoveries of all the learned men of all the ages. (C. H. SPURGEON)

More Precious than Gold

Even more important than what men think of the Word of God is what God says about His own Word. According to the Bible, the Word of the Lord is true (Psalms 33:4; 119:160); it is pure (Psalms 12:6; 19:9; 119:140 KJV; Proverbs 30:5 KJV); it is righteous and fully trustworthy (Psalm 119:138); it is eternal and stands firm in the heavens (Psalm 119:89); it is divinely inspired (2 Timothy 3:16 KJV; 2 Peter 1:21); it is profitable for our lives and walk (2 Timothy 3:16); it is perfect (Psalm 19:7); it is of greater value than any amount of gold or silver (Psalm 119:72); it is sweet to the taste (Psalms 19:10; 119:103; Ezekiel 3:3).

The power and authority of God's Word infinitely surpass that of any other book that has ever been written. As a troubled young seminary professor being pursued by the "Hound of Heaven," Martin Luther experienced the supernatural, transforming power of the Word that later led him to write, "The Bible is alive, it speaks to me; it has feet, it runs after me; it has hands, it lays hold on me."

When we pick up a copy of the Bible, do we realize what it is that we are holding in our hands? Do we ever stop to think that this is actually the *Word of God*? As Augustine reminds us, "When the Bible speaks, *God* speaks!" In the West we have been blessed with such easy access to the Word that it is hard not to take it for granted.

Margaret Nikol remembers vividly what it was like not to

have access to a Bible. A concert violinist, Margaret grew up in Bulgaria under one of Communism's most repressive regimes. Though her father was a pastor, he did not own a Bible. When she was a little girl, the Communists confiscated virtually all the Bibles in the country.

However, an elderly woman in Margaret's town managed to hold on to one Bible, which became a treasure shared by all the believers in the town—literally. Each page was carefully torn out of the Bible and distributed one by one. Margaret felt blessed to receive one page that included Genesis 16 and 17—a page she cherished and diligently studied. Her brother, a pastor in Bulgaria, had as his sole "library" a couple of pages from the Bible that he had copied by hand.

When Margaret was in her midthirties, she was exiled to the United States. Shortly after she arrived in America, some newfound friends asked what she would like for Christmas. Margaret didn't have to think long. More than anything else, she wanted a Bible.

Margaret describes the day her friends took her to a Christian bookstore to make the purchase. It was the very first time she had ever seen a complete Bible: "There were red ones and black ones and green ones and blue ones and brown ones— every size, every shape—Bibles everywhere!" Overwhelmed by the sight, the thirty-seven-year-old woman stood in the aisle of that bookstore and "wept and wept and wept for joy!"

It is impossible for most of us to imagine what Margaret felt at that moment. A recent count in my personal library revealed more than thirty copies of the Bible—red, black, green, blue, and brown—every size, every shape—in at least eight different translations. That doesn't include a host of commentaries, concordances, reference books, devotional books, and hymnals.

Proverbs tells us that "he who is full loathes honey, but to the hungry even what is bitter tastes sweet" (27:7). To hungry souls in parts of the world that have never been allowed to own a Bible, the Word of God is exceedingly precious. But to those of us who can turn on the radio and hear the Word preached every hour of the day, who can walk into any bookstore and find the Bible of our choice, who have Bibles located every several inches on the backs of our pews, and whose shelves are bursting with Bibles, some of them unused—we may find ourselves in danger of adopting a casual attitude toward the Word of God.

If you have ever traveled in the Middle East, you are probably familiar with the utmost reverence that Muslims accord to their holy book, the Qur'an. You will never see them placing a copy of the Qur'an on the floor or treating it casually. Rather, the Qur'an is to be kept above the level of their heads and above all other books in the room. They treat their holy book with great care, keeping it wrapped in a special cloth and placing it on a special stand when they wish to read it. They believe that every word in the book is holy and that it should be highly respected.

The Scripture says that God has exalted His Word above even His own name (Psalm 138:2 KJV). If God esteems His Word that highly, what should be our attitude toward the Word? In Psalm 119, David speaks of loving the Word, reverencing it, delighting in it, longing for it, trusting it, and fearing it. God says through the prophet Isaiah, "This is the one I esteem: he who is humble and contrite in spirit, and *trembles* at my word" (Isaiah 66:2, emphasis added; cf. Psalm 119:161). What does it mean to tremble at the Word of the Lord? It means to have an attitude of reverential awe and fear. It is the opposite of a cavalier attitude toward the Word.

My father had a great reverence and love for the Word of God. As a way of demonstrating that respect, it was his habit never to place anything on top of the Bible—a practice I have adopted myself, not because the pulp and leather have any mystical properties or inherent value, but as a visible means of honoring what is contained in those pages.

Our Most Valuable Treasure

In Psalm 119, David can scarcely contain his joy as he rehearses the blessings and benefits he has received from the Word of God.

We learn that the Word of God has power to keep us from sin (Psalm 119:9, 11), to strengthen us when we are grieving (v. 28), to comfort us when we are suffering (vv. 50, 52), to grant us freedom (v. 45), to give us understanding and light for our path (v. 104), and to give us peace and keep us from stumbling (v. 165).

The Word of God will light your way; it will help you make right choices; it will heal your wounds and settle your heart; it will warn you of danger; it will protect and cleanse you from sin; it will lead you; it will make you wise. It is bread; it is water; it is a counselor; it is life. It is satisfying; it is sufficient; it is supreme; it is supernatural. The hymn writer put it this way:

> Holy Bible, book divine,
>   Precious treasure, thou art mine;
> Mine to tell me whence I came;
>   Mine to teach me what I am.
>
> Mine to chide me when I rove;
>   Mine to show a Savior's love;
> Mine thou art to guide and guard;
>   Mine to punish or reward.
>
> Mine to comfort in distress,
>   Suff'ring in this wilderness;
> Mine to show, by living faith,
>   Man can triumph over death.
>
> Mine to tell of joys to come,
>   And the rebel sinner's doom;
> O thou Holy Book divine,
>   Precious treasure, thou art mine.
>
> —JOHN BURTON (1773–1822)

reparation Matters!

If you know you have an important meeting with your boss and the owner of the company first thing tomorrow morning, when do you begin preparing for it? Do you wait until after you get up in the morning, until after you have exercised, showered, dressed, and eaten, before you start thinking about getting ready for your meeting? Do you all of a sudden look at your watch, realize the meeting has already begun, grab some crumpled clothes out of the dirty laundry, throw them on as you race to the car, arrive thirty minutes late to the meeting, sit down at the table where the others are already assembled, and then hastily start scribbling out notes for your presentation? Not if you care about your job.

When you announce to your small children that the family is going to take a trip to visit their favorite uncle when school gets out in two weeks, do they forget about it until it's time to get in the car to leave? If your children are like some children I know, they have their suitcases packed a week ahead of time! They plan out exactly what they are going to do with the cousins; they want to draw pictures for Uncle Monty and Aunt Suzy—you can hardly get them to think about anything else.

Years ago, while taking cello lessons, I learned that when I picked up the instrument, if I immediately began to play, the result was sure to be unpleasant to the ears. First I had to tighten the bow and lubricate it with resin. Then the height of the cello had to be adjusted correctly. Then each string had to be tuned. All these preparations directly affected the outcome of my playing.

When I agreed not long ago to host a special dinner in my home, I immediately began making preparations—I had lists of my lists. I spent the better part of three days just getting ready for those guests.

Whether for a critical meeting, a family vacation, making music, or hosting guests, preparation is essential. Preparation is no less crucial to meeting with God and cultivating a relationship with Him through His Word.

In fact, I have found that one of the greatest hindrances to a meaningful quiet time is the failure to have a prepared heart. Hour after hour throughout each day, our eyes and ears are lured by the world around us. The sights, sounds, and demands of our surroundings have a way of capturing our minds and hearts. That is why we often find ourselves distracted, hurried, and having quiet times with hearts that are far from quiet. A little bit of preparation can make a big difference.

BEGIN THE NIGHT BEFORE

Some of those preparations are very practical. For example, it helps me to keep my Bible, journal, pen, devotional books, hymnal, and other tools (more about those in chapter 9) together in the place where I am planning to meet with the Lord in the morning. If I have to run around gathering those items, valuable time will be lost and my mind will be distracted before I even begin.

As much as possible, I try to prepare for the next day the night before, so my mind can be free to concentrate on the Lord in the morning. (I am not naturally an organized person, but I have found that disciplining myself to plan ahead can greatly enhance the quality of the time I spend alone with the Lord. Although those habits don't come easily to me, they are well worth the effort to develop.)

As we pointed out in the last chapter, another key to success in meeting God in the morning is to get to bed early enough the night before. Most of us are not physically able to stay up until the middle of the night and then be alert and attentive to the Lord early in the morning—certainly not on any kind of regular basis. Getting to bed at a reasonable hour may require putting the children to bed earlier, limiting late-night engagements and social events, taking fewer evening commitments, getting chores done earlier in the evening, or turning off the television. Speaking of which . . .

If the last thing on our minds at night is the raucous sound

of late-night entertainment on television, we are not likely to
awaken the next morning prepared and eager to seek the
Lord. As an alternative, why not try playing a tape of quiet, in-
strumental songs of worship and praise as the family is
preparing for bed? (By the way, maintaining a calm, worshipful
atmosphere at home in the evening may help your children
sleep more peacefully at night, as well as cause them to have a
more settled spirit in the morning.)

Devoting our final waking moments to meditating on the
Lord and His Word is another way to prepare for our meeting
with Him in the morning.

Psalm 4 may well be a prayer that David prayed before he
went to sleep at night. Notice that even though he is in the
midst of stressful circumstances, there is no panic in his tone;
rather, his spirit is serene as he directs his thoughts heavenward:

> When you are on your beds,
>   search your hearts and be silent.
> Offer right sacrifices
>   and trust in the LORD.
>
> . . . Let the light of your face shine upon us, O LORD.
> You have filled my heart with greater joy
>   than when their grain and new wine abound.
> I will lie down and sleep in peace,
>   for you alone, O LORD,
>   make me dwell in safety.
>
> —PSALM 4:4–8

There are other prayers in the Psalms that I can imagine
David voicing to the Lord just before his eyes closed in sleep at
night:

> How precious to me are your thoughts, O God!
> How vast is the sum of them!

> Were I to count them,
>> they would outnumber the grains of sand.
> When I awake,
>> I am still with you.
>
> —PSALM 139:17–18

> In righteousness I will see your face;
>> when I awake, I will be satisfied with seeing your likeness.
>
> —PSALM 17:15

Before falling asleep at night, you may want to pray something like this: "Father, by Your Spirit, please minister to my spirit through the night. As I sleep, fill my subconscious mind with thoughts of Jesus. And may I awake beholding His likeness—thinking of and loving Him, satisfied with You and prepared to seek Your face."

When the Alarm Goes Off

Brrrriinnnnggg! As soon as that alarm clock sounds, we are faced with an important choice. (I'm assuming another crucial choice was made the night before: to set the alarm early enough to allow for unhurried time with the Lord before having to begin the rest of the day's business.)

What we do in those first moments of wakefulness will either help or hinder us in cultivating intimacy during our time alone with the Lord.

You may be one of those people whose first response to the sound of the alarm is to push the "reality delayer" (a.k.a. snooze button)—somehow, at that moment, a few more minutes of sleep seems a lot more appealing than digging into the Word.

Or, if you're like me, as soon as your eyes open, you begin to think about all the things you have to do that day. As soon as you are on your feet, you are immediately tempted to begin attending to unfinished tasks around the house. (This is a particular danger for me, as my office is in my home and the "to do" piles never seem to go away!)

Puritan pastor Lewis Bayly encouraged a different choice and explained why it is so important to turn the heart to the Lord before doing anything else in the morning:

> As soon as ever thou awakest in the morning, keep the door of thy heart fast shut, that no earthly thought may enter, before that God come in first. And let Him, before all others, have the first place there. So all evil thoughts either will not dare to come in, or shall the easier be kept out; and the heart will more savour of piety and godliness all the day after; but if thy heart be not, at thy first waking, filled with some meditations of God and His word . . . , Satan will attempt to fill it with worldly cares or fleshly desires, so that it will grow unfit for the service of God all the day after. . . .
>
> Begin, therefore, every day's work with God's word and prayer . . . and as soon as thou awakest say to Him thus: My soul waiteth on Thee, O Lord, more than the morning watch watcheth for the morning! O God, therefore be merciful unto me, and bless me, and cause thy face to shine upon me! Fill me with Thy mercy this morning, so shall I rejoice and be glad all my days.[2]

Tuning the Heart

What Bayly was suggesting is that our hearts need to be "tuned" to the Lord, much as a musical instrument needs to be tuned to an absolute pitch before it can make beautiful music. Over the years, I have used various means to get my heart in tune with His.

The words of Isaiah 50:4–5 have often helped to tune my heart; many times, even before getting out of bed in the morning, I have meditated on this passage and prayed it back to the Lord:

> *The Sovereign LORD has given me an instructed tongue,*
> *to know the word that sustains the weary.*

"Lord God, You are my Lord. You are the sovereign God. I want You to reign in my life this day. I know that today You will bring people into my life—family members, friends, fellow workers, people I don't even know—people who are weary and need a word from You to sustain and encourage them. I will not know how to speak the words they need to hear, unless You first instruct me."

> *He wakens me morning by morning,*
> *wakens my ear to listen like one being taught.*

"Thank You, Lord, for waking me this morning. Before I can teach others, I must be taught by You. Before I open my mouth to speak to others, I need to listen to You. Please open my ears to hear what You want to say to me this day."

> *The Sovereign LORD has opened my ears,*
> *and I have not been rebellious;*
> *I have not drawn back.*

"As You speak to me, may my heart be submissive toward You. May I not resist anything that You say to me today."

Frequently, I will read one or two selections from a devotional book as a means of tuning my heart before I open the Scripture. These books, written by human authors, should never take the place of the Word of God itself, but they can help us focus on spiritual matters and clear out any clutter that may be distracting us. (In the Appendix, you will find a list of devotional books that have been of particular blessing to me over the years.)

Hymns that express a longing and a desire to hear the voice of God can be another means of getting our hearts in tune. Try reading or singing one or more of these hymns to the Lord:

> Speak, Lord, in the stillness,
> While I wait on Thee;

Hushed my heart to listen
In expectancy.

Speak, O blessed Master.
In this quiet hour;
Let me see Thy face, Lord,
Feel Thy touch of power.

For the words Thou speakest,
They are life indeed;
Living bread from heaven,
Now my spirit feed!

—E. MAY GRIMES (1868–1927)[3]

Open my eyes, that I may see
Glimpses of truth Thou hast for me;
Place in my hands the wonderful key,
That shall unclasp and set me free.
Silently now I wait for Thee,
Ready, my God, Thy will to see;
Open my eyes, illumine me,
Spirit divine!

—CLARA H. SCOTT (1841–97)

Now, with hearts tuned and spiritual ears and eyes attentive to Him, we open the pages of that wondrous Book, there expecting to encounter its Author and to be transformed in His presence.

MAKING IT PERSONAL

1. Plan a time into your schedule when you can read aloud through Psalm 119 in one sitting. You may want to do this alone, or as a family, or with a group of friends. The psalm is divided into twenty-two eight-verse stanzas. Have each individual read one stanza in succession until you have read through the entire psalm.

2. Now look back over Psalm 119 and make a list of the characteristics of the Word of God and the benefits and blessings that it is intended to bring to our lives.

3. Write a prayer thanking the Lord for His Word and for what it has meant in your life.

4. Record two or three practical steps you could take to better prepare your heart to receive the Word each day.

FROM THE HEART OF
Tina Norviel

I am grateful that as a teenager I promised the Lord I would be in His Word every day, unless providentially hindered. That promise has kept me walking with Him daily. I don't decide each day whether or not I am going to get up and meet with God—I made that choice a long time ago. It has become so much a part of my life that I would no more think of beginning a day without spending time with the Lord than I would skip brushing my teeth or getting dressed! A firm commitment to "just do it" is so crucial.

Without a consistent devotional life, I am out of vital contact with my only true Source of strength, guidance, encouragement, conviction, joy, love, grace—all that I must have to live for and be like Him.

Probably the biggest obstacle to my meeting with God is my own laziness in the area of concentration and focus. During my reading or prayer time, it amazes me how quickly I can be thinking about a dozen other things. When I realize what has happened, I seek God's forgiveness, yield back control of my mind to Him, and ask for His help.

I have found that my mind is more likely to wander if I do not use an organized prayer list. I divide the names of those I pray for into days of the week, so that I pray for most people weekly. Then I have a list of people and special burdens and needs that I pray for daily. I also ask God to bring special requests to my mind as I pray.

By far, my greatest joy is spending time adoring the Lamb of God for His sacrifice on the cross. The section of hymns on the cross in my hymnal is a wonderful means to express my worship to the Lamb. Nothing drives me to repentance and surrender like this time of meditation and adoration of Christ as the Lamb of God. In times of selfishness or discouragement, this exercise quickly encourages my heart.

Tina Norviel and her husband, John, served on the staff of Life Action Ministries for ten years. They currently live in Salt Lake City, Utah, where John is planting a church and Tina home-schools their two children.

NOTES

PART PAGE: Oswald J. Smith, *The Man God Uses* (Burlington, Ontario: Welch, 1984), 74.

PART PAGE: George Müller, in *Spiritual Secrets of George Müller*, ed. Roger Steer (Wheaton: Harold Shaw, 1985), 60–61.

1. This story is recounted in *Mary Jones and Her Bible*, by M. E. R. (England: Gospel Standard Trust, 1996). Charles Thomas's encounter with Mary Jones deeply impressed him and led to the establishment in 1804 of the British and Foreign Bible Society, a society dedicated to publishing and distributing the Word of God throughout the world.

2. Lewis Bayly, *The Practice of Piety* (1842; reprint, Morgan, Pa.: Soli Deo Gloria, 1995), 102.

3. "Speak, Lord, in the Stillness," lyrics by E. May Grimes, setting by Alfred B. Smith. Copyright 1951 Singspiration Music/ASCAP. All rights reserved. Reprinted by special permission of Brentwood-Benson Music Publishing, Inc.

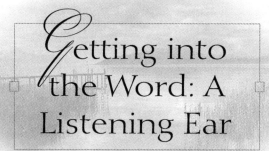

CHAPTER 8

Getting into the Word: A Listening Ear

We have all heard people say that they just can't understand the Bible or that they don't get anything out of it. In my experience, one of the biggest reasons the Bible remains a mystery to people is because they don't read it. With tongue in cheek, one writer suggested that "if all the neglected Bibles were dusted simultaneously, we would have a record dust storm and the sun would go into eclipse for a whole week!"

God promises a blessing to those who read His Word (Revelation 1:3). At the beginning of their reigns, the kings of Israel were commanded to write out by hand a copy of the Law of God; then they were to read that copy every day for the rest of their lives, so they would learn to fear the Lord and keep His commandments (Deuteronomy 17:18–20). Through His prophet Isaiah, God commanded the Israelites, "Look in the scroll of the LORD and read" (Isaiah 34:16). On more than one occasion in the Old Testament, revival broke out when God's people began to read His Word that had been neglected (Nehemiah 8–10; 2 Chronicles 34:14–33).

The Gospels record several instances where Jesus turned to His critics and said, "Haven't you read in the Law . . . ?" "Have you never read in the Scriptures . . . ?" (Matthew 12:5; 21:42; cf. 12:3; 19:4; 21:16). In other words, He expected them to have read and applied the Scripture, and when they needed to be corrected, He sent them right back to the Word of God.

It was while the Ethiopian official was reading the scroll of the book of Isaiah that his eyes were opened and God gave his heart repentance, faith, and salvation (Acts 8:27–39).

When the apostle Paul sent his divinely inspired letter to the church at Colossae, he wanted to be sure that the believers read not only that letter, but also the one he had sent to the believers in Laodicea (Colossians 4:16). Likewise, he said to the Thessalonians, "I charge you before the Lord to have this letter read to all the brothers" (1 Thessalonians 5:27). Paul exhorted the young pastor Timothy to make the public reading of Scripture a high priority (1 Timothy 4:13).

Oswald Chambers emphasized the importance of reading the Scripture:

> The mere reading of the Word of God has power to communicate the life of God to us mentally, morally and spiritually. God makes the words of the Bible a sacrament, i.e., the means whereby we partake of His life; it is one of His secret doors for the communication of His life to us.

Read Prayerfully

As you read, ask God to give you understanding. Ask Him to open up to you those portions that are difficult to grasp. Ask Him to make familiar passages fresh and alive to your heart. Ask Him to reveal Himself, His heart, and His ways to you.

William Gurnall was a devout minister in England during the seventeenth century. He wrote of the need to read the Scripture prayerfully:

Go to God by prayer for a key to unlock the mysteries of His word. It is not the plodding but the praying soul, that will get this treasure of scripture knowledge. God often brings a truth to the Christian's hand as a return of prayer, which he had long hunted for in vain with much labour and study: "There is a God in heaven that revealeth secrets" (Daniel 2:28); and where doth He reveal the secrets of His word but at the throne of grace?[1]

A practice that has made an enormous difference in my own devotional life is that of beginning my time in the Word each day by thoughtfully praying these words of Scripture back to the Lord:

> *Open my eyes that I may see*
> *wonderful things in your law. . . .*
> *Give me understanding, and I will keep your law*
> *and obey it with all my heart. . . .*
>
> *Show me your ways, O LORD,*
> *teach me your paths;*
> *guide me in your truth and teach me,*
> *for you are God my Savior,*
> *and my hope is in you all day long. . . .*
>
> *That which I see not teach thou me: if I have done iniquity, I*
> *will do no more.*
>
> —PSALM 119:18, 34; 25:4–5; JOB 34:32 KJV

God has been gracious to make the Word come alive to me as I take time to pray that prayer each morning. As I pray those words, I am expressing two things to the Lord.

First, I am acknowledging that this is not an ordinary Book I am about to read, but a *supernatural,* and, therefore, I need the assistance of its Author. A. W. Tozer reminds us, "The Bible is a supernatural book and can be understood only by supernatural aid."

Jesus told His disciples He was going to send His Holy Spirit as a Counselor to teach them and to guide them into all truth (John 14:26). First Corinthians 2:14 tells us that the natural man cannot understand the things of God. Only the Spirit of God can open them up to us. James says, "If any of you lacks wisdom, he should ask God, who gives generously to all without finding fault, and it will be given to him" (1:5).

"Even the Bible," said Coleridge, "without the Holy Spirit, is like a sundial by moonlight." We need the Holy Spirit, who inspired this book, to give us wisdom and understanding, to be our teacher, and to shed divine light on the Word.

Second—and this is so important—I am committing to God, ahead of the fact, that whatever He says to me through His Word I will obey. "I will hasten and not delay to obey your commands," the psalmist declared (Psalm 119:60). "Give me understanding, and I will keep your law and obey it with all my heart" (Psalm 119:34). I am saying to God, "Please speak to me; and whatever You say, whether I like it or not, whether I agree with it or not, whether it is easy or not, whether or not it fits my preconceived notions, by Your enabling grace and power, *I will obey.*"

Frances Ridley Havergal, the beloved nineteenth-century hymn writer, expressed her commitment to obey whatever God said to her through His Word:

> Master, speak! and make me ready,
> When Thy voice is truly heard,
> With obedience glad and steady,
> Still to follow every word.

Read Thoughtfully

When we were teens, one of the skills my dad encouraged us to acquire was speed-reading. However, he suggested that there were two things which should never be speed-read: love letters and the Bible. Most of us wouldn't think of hastily skimming through a love letter. On the contrary, we pore over its contents and read and reread them, searching for every nuance of meaning we can possibly glean from between the lines.

In fact, the Bible is a "love letter"; it reveals God's heart to us, and the more carefully, frequently, and thoughtfully we read it, the more we will grasp of His loving heart and intentions toward us.

Those who read the Bible hastily or casually will never mine its riches and plumb its depths for themselves. Psalm 19 tells us that the Word of God is "more precious than gold, than much pure gold" (v. 10). Generally speaking, you don't walk down the street and stumble onto vast stores of gold. Gold is a precious, rare commodity that is buried deep in the earth. Those who wish to own gold must expend significant time and effort to search for it and to extract it from the rock in which it is embedded.

During his forty-year reign as the king of Israel, Solomon sent envoys far and wide throughout the earth in search of priceless treasures. He also understood the importance of searching earnestly for the wealth of God's ways. That is why he wrote to his son:

> *If you call out for insight*
> *and cry aloud for understanding,*
> *and if you look for it as for silver*
> *and search for it as for hidden treasure,*
> *then you will understand the fear of the LORD*
> *and find the knowledge of God.*
>
> —PROVERBS 2:3–5

As you read, pause frequently to meditate on the meaning of what you are reading. Absorb the Word into your system by dwelling on it, pondering it, going over it again and again in your mind, considering it from many different angles, until it becomes a part of *you*. The Puritan Thomas Watson spoke of the necessity of meditation:

Without meditation the truths which we know will never affect our hearts. . . . As an hammer drives a nail to the head, so meditation drives a truth to the heart. . . . Read before you meditate. "Give attendance to reading" (1 Timothy 4:13). Then it follows, "meditate upon these things" (v. 15). Reading doth furnish with matter; it is the oil that feeds the lamp of meditation. Be sure your meditations are founded upon Scripture. Reading without meditation is unfruitful; meditation without reading is dangerous.[2]

One of the most valuable aids to meditation is Scripture memorization. In fact, when I encounter someone who is battling discouragement or depression, I often ask two questions: "Are you singing to the Lord?" and "Are you memorizing Scripture?" These two exercises are not some magical formula to make all our problems go away, but they do have incredible power to change our perspective and attitude toward the issues we are facing.

"But I can't memorize," some will quickly respond. Don Whitney points out that the issue is not so much our ability to memorize as our motivation:

What if I offered you one thousand dollars for every verse you could memorize in the next seven days? Do you think your attitude toward Scripture memory and your ability to memorize would improve? Any financial reward would be minimal when compared to the accumulating value of the treasure of God's Word deposited within your mind.[3]

The fact is, we can and do memorize all the time. We memorize people's names, television commercials, directions to places we frequent, credit card numbers, and phone numbers. How? We remember information that is important to us or that we frequently use or repeat. Scripture memorization is no different. It requires motivation and regular, systematic review.

If you have not memorized Scripture before, start with small portions, perhaps one or two verses a week. Select verses that relate to specific concerns or needs in your life. You may want to write out the verses on a card that you can keep with you and review several times a day. Reviewing Scripture before going to sleep at night is one of the best ways to reinforce it in your memory.

Once you have mastered a verse or a paragraph, go on to the next, but review daily the verses you have memorized most recently. You may find it helpful to memorize with a partner so that you can encourage each other and check up on each other's verses on a regular basis.

Scripture memory and meditation will bring about many benefits in your life, including

- cleansing and renewing your mind;
- keeping you from sin;
- providing insight and direction in the midst of real-life situations;
- strengthening your spirit;
- combating the attacks of the Enemy on your mind and emotions;
- stimulating spiritual desires;
- diminishing the demands of your flesh;
- protecting you from wrong thinking patterns; and
- fixing your mind and affections on "things above" (Colossians 3:2).

Evidence Not Seen is the moving story of Darlene Deibler Rose, a young American missionary who spent four years in a Japanese prison camp during World War II. She recalls the way God used Scriptures she had memorized as a child to sustain her through her terrifying ordeal:

As a child and young person, I had had a driving compulsion to memorize the written Word. In the cell I was grateful now for those days in Vacation Bible School, when I had memorized many single verses, complete chapters, and Psalms, as well as whole books of the Bible. In the years that followed, I reviewed the Scriptures often. The Lord fed me with the Living Bread that had been stored against the day when fresh supply was cut off by the loss of my Bible. He brought daily comfort and encouragement—yes, and joy—to my heart through the knowledge of the Word. . . . I had never needed the Scriptures more than in these months on death row, but since so much of His Word was there in my heart, it was not the punishment the Kempeitai had anticipated when they took my Bible.[4]

Read Systematically

As I was writing this afternoon, I took a break to go make myself a sandwich. Can you imagine if I had opened the refrigerator, closed my eyes, and grabbed whatever items my hand happened to reach first? Instead of a peanut butter and jelly sandwich, I might have ended up with a plate of onions, mustard, and whipped cream—not especially appetizing or nourishing. Yet that is a picture of the way many people approach the Word of God. They blindly "grab" whatever passage they come to first, in no particular sequence or order. When passages are separated from their context, their meaning is changed and well-meaning believers can easily be misled.

Others read the Bible much like a teenager whose preferred diet consists of pizza, chips, pop, and ice cream. Our bodies require a nutritionally balanced diet in order to stay healthy. Likewise, our spirits need the balance that comes from taking in the "whole counsel of God," not limiting ourselves to those passages that seem particularly appetizing. The spiritual growth of some believers has been stunted due to a diet that consists primarily of the Psalms with perhaps a smidgen of the New Testament Epistles.

It is true that not all parts of the Bible are equally easy to digest. This week I have been reading in 1 Chronicles and Ezekiel. Unlike the "succulent" passages we might discover in 1 Peter or the gospel of John, there are some passages in those books that seem particularly tedious and even unnecessary. Even the great Puritan pastor John Bunyan admitted, "I have sometimes seen more in a line of the Bible than I could well tell how to stand under, and yet at another time the whole Bible hath been to me as dry as a stick."

But Paul reminded Timothy that "*all* Scripture is God-breathed and is useful for teaching, rebuking, correcting and training in righteousness" (2 Timothy 3:16, emphasis added). That means we need a diet that includes *all* of God's Word.

One problem is that we have become so accustomed to having our senses titillated by visual and audible thrills that we are easily bored by anything that does not yield immediate excitement and rewards. Oswald Chambers wisely pointed out that "the Bible does not thrill, the Bible nourishes. Give time to the reading of the Bible and the recreating effect is as real as that of fresh air physically."

Another author put it this way:

> The Bible resembles an extensive and highly cultivated garden, where there is a vast variety and profusion of fruits and flowers: some of which are more essential or more splendid than others; but there is not a blade suffered to grow in it, which has not its use and beauty in the system.[5]

Yes, we need the Psalms and the Epistles. But we also need the Books of the Law, the Historical Books, the Prophets, and the Gospels. We need the whole of God's Word. And we need to read in such a way that we get a sense of the flow of the Word.

When we pick up a book, we don't generally start in the middle and jump around haphazardly from chapter to chapter—especially if the book has a plot. But that is exactly the way many of us read the Word of God. We have failed to see that the Bible has a plot, that it is one grand story that has a beginning and a conclusion. It is the story of redemption—the story of a God who created man for fellowship with Himself, watched as man rejected His overtures, and then stooped down to restore man to intimacy with Himself through the Cross.

The fact that the Bible is a whole doesn't mean it can only be read straight through, from Genesis to Revelation, although many believers find great blessing in doing this on a regular basis. It does mean that context and flow are important. Individual verses need to be read in the context of the paragraph and chapter in which they appear. Chapters should be studied in light of the entire book where they are found. And the various books make more sense if we understand how they fit into the scheme and flow of the Bible and God's eternal, redemptive plan.

If you want to get a balanced spiritual diet as well as an understanding of the whole plan of God, make sure that you are not overlooking or bypassing certain portions of the Word.

DIFFERENT APPROACHES

There are many different ways to read the Bible systematically. There are numerous Bible reading plans available today, some designed to help you read through the entire Bible in a year, others in a longer time span.

The Daily Walk, published by Walk Thru the Bible Ministries, is an excellent resource for reading through the Bible in a year.[6] The Bible is divided into daily portions (an average of three to four chapters per day will take you through the Bible in a year) with a page of helpful notes and practical insights to shed additional light on the passage for that day. *Closer Walk*, also available from Walk Thru the Bible, takes the reader through the New Testament in one year.

Personally, I generally prefer to read in both the Old and New Testaments at the same time. There are several reasons for this: First, the Old Testament sheds light on the New and vice versa. Those connections are easier to see when I am reading in both Testaments. Second, I don't like to go for long periods of time without reading in the Gospels. That is where we get the clearest picture of the Lord Jesus. If the goal of our devotional life is to know Him and to be conformed to His image, then we will want to go back to the Gospels over and over again. Third, by reading in both Testaments, the more difficult Old Testament passages are balanced out with other portions that are easier to "digest."

My father had an approach to Bible reading that he rarely varied. Each morning he read five chapters from the Psalms and one from the Proverbs, thus reading through the Psalms and Proverbs every month. Then he read two chapters consecutively from the Old Testament and one from the New.

Some time ago, a dear, older servant of the Lord recommended an approach to Bible reading that I have found to be a great blessing. He suggested dividing the Bible into six major sections, beginning in Genesis, Joshua, Job, Isaiah, Matthew, and Romans. Each day, read one or more chapters consecutively in each of those sections. Mark where you end up in each section so you can pick up at that location the next day.

This has been one of the most exciting ways I have discovered to read the Word. Though penned by many different authors over a period of fifteen hundred years, there is a unity and coherence in the Scripture that can only be supernatural. Invariably, I find that what I am reading in one portion dovetails precisely with what I am reading in another.

At times you may feel the need to take a particular book or section of the Bible and "place it under a microscope." One way of doing that is to take a specific book of the Bible and read through it every day for thirty days. This is a good way to gain deeper insight into the heart and message of an individual book.

You will probably find that your devotional life stays fresher if you vary your approach to Bible reading from time to time. At times, you may want to read just a small portion each day, meditating on each word and phrase. During other seasons, you may choose to cover more ground more quickly, looking for the broader, overarching themes. Occasionally, you may wish to take a break from reading consecutively in order to focus on a particular topic, word, or character from the

Bible. However, it is wise not to neglect systematic reading of the Scripture for any length of time.

Periodically I have found great value in reading through the Scripture at a more rapid pace, so as to gain a greater understanding and appreciation for the whole of God's Word.

This past year, I have read through the entire Bible three times—a faster pace than I normally prefer—in order to get a bird's-eye view of the panoramic plan of God. The view has been magnificent—much like the spectacular vista from a mountain peak thousands of feet above the earth. There are themes that run like rivers from Genesis to Revelation—at points they are just a trickle; at other places they become a powerful, gushing force.

Like threads in a great tapestry, those themes are woven together to form the matchless story of Redemption. God's plan to create and redeem a race for Himself; His unending love, mercy, and grace; His long-suffering toward sinners, and yet His righteous judgment against those who refuse to repent; the wiles and persistent, relentless hatred and rebellion of Satan against God; Satan's never-ending attempts to persuade man to join him in his sedition; God's ultimate, decisive triumph over Satan and His eternal rule over heaven and earth and hell—these are some of the overarching views that have filled my vision as I have looked at the Scripture as a whole.

Reading the Bible in this way has given me greater understanding and appreciation of the ways of God. For example, as I have walked with both Old and New Testament saints, I have seen that faith pleases God. Through those seemingly endless Old Testament laws and instructions concerning the offering of sacrifices, I have been reminded that sin is costly and that it can be atoned for only by a blood sacrifice. As I have moved from the old to the new covenant, I have heard the sweet music of the gospel—the glad refrain that the blood of Jesus, the spotless Lamb of God, satisfies the wrath of God against sin and cleanses the sinner's guilty conscience.

On virtually every page of this Book I have seen the likeness and the signature of the Lord Jesus. I have marveled and wondered and wept at the glory of His presence, at His redeeming love, at the spectacle of the cross, and at the hope that is ours through Him.

Don't Get Discouraged!

As meaningful as the Scripture has been to me through this journey, I want to be quick to say that not every day or every portion has been a spiritual feast, any more than every meal I eat is a scrumptious banquet. Some passages have tasted more like cardboard than honey! Some days, I have felt like I was trudging through mud, rather than "walking on the King's highway." (Even the apostle Peter acknowledged that some of Paul's writings were "hard to understand"—2 Peter 3:16.)

However, the value and impact of the Word in our lives cannot necessarily be seen in one day's or one week's intake. When a child is growing up, you don't usually see evidence of physical growth on a daily basis. But gradually you realize that his pants are getting shorter and his arms are protruding out of his shirtsleeves. At the end of the year, when that child stands up against the same wall where you measured his height last year, you are amazed to realize how much he has grown.

Likewise, the value of a balanced, nutritious diet is not generally experienced in one day or one week; rather, the cumulative benefits of eating right will be experienced over an extended period of time.

In much the same way, the spiritual value and growth we receive from the Word will be evident, not so much from one day to the next as when we stop and look back over a period of months or years and realize the extent to which the Word has shaped and molded our lives. (It is equally true that the effects of poor eating habits are not usually seen overnight; so the consequences of a poor spiritual diet may not be immediately apparent—but they definitely will be evident in the long run.)

Therefore, when you come across portions of Scripture that seem to make no sense or have no apparent value (and you will), don't give up. And don't conclude that those portions are worthless. Oswald Chambers exhorts:

> *Read* the Bible, whether you understand it or not, and the Holy Spirit will bring back some word of Jesus to you in a particular set of circumstances and make it living.

Remember that whether we understand it or not, whether it is easy reading or not, the Word of God is still profitable—*all* of it (2 Timothy 3:16). Unlike any other book that has ever been written, the Bible is alive; and it comes with a personal Tutor—the Holy Spirit who lives in us. His job is to teach us what we need to know and to give us understanding into spiritual truth that we cannot perceive with our natural minds.

Even those passages that are most difficult to grasp or seem to be of relatively little value have a sanctifying effect as they enter into our spirit. Jesus said to His disciples, "Now ye are clean through the word which I have spoken unto you" (John 15:3 KJV). Often after I have finished reading a portion for the day, I will pray and ask the Lord to cleanse my spirit, my heart, my mind, and my life with the water of His Word (Ephesians 5:26).

Don't Forget the Goal!

Whatever approach you take to reading the Bible, don't let yourself become a slave to the method. Don't get so caught up in the mechanics that you miss the point.

Remember that the goal is not how fast you can get through the Bible. The goal is to get the Word into your heart and life and to cultivate an intimate relationship with Jesus, the living Word of God. It is possible to "know" the Word intellectually from cover to cover while failing to see and know Jesus, the living "Word" of God.

One of the most sobering passages in the Bible has to do with this concern. The Pharisees of Jesus' day were renowned

for their vast, superior knowledge of the Old Testament Scriptures. Yet one day Jesus looked them squarely in the eye and
said, *"You have never heard [the Father's] voice nor seen his form, nor does
his word dwell in you"* (John 5:37–38 emphasis added).

I can just see those indignant, bedecked Bible scholars
turning red in the face and spluttering under their breath:
"What does he mean? Who does he think he is? He's just a
blue-collar worker! He's never even been to seminary! And *he's*
telling *us* that we have never heard God speak and that His
Word doesn't dwell in us? Why, we've spent our whole lives
mastering the Bible! If *we* haven't heard God's voice, who has?"

But Jesus wasn't finished. He went on: "You diligently study
the Scriptures because you think that by them you possess
eternal life. These are the Scriptures that testify about *me*, yet
you refuse to come to *me* to have life" (John 5:39–40, emphasis
added).

What was Jesus saying? He wanted those men to understand that they had missed the whole point of Bible study. The
purpose of getting into the Word of God is to meet Jesus. *He* is
the object of our pursuit; He *is* the Word! It's all about *Him*. If
we master the Bible but don't end up knowing, loving, worshiping, serving, and being like Jesus, we are really no better
than the devil himself.

Press On to the Top

One of my favorite vacation spots is in western Wyoming,
near the majestic Grand Teton mountains. A few years ago, I
stayed in a home on a mountain that faces the Tetons. Early
one morning, I left the house to walk up the mountain. Fog
had settled in over the area and the entire Teton Range seemed
to have disappeared.

In spite of the fact that the view was much less than spectacular, I began what for me was a moderately difficult climb
up the mountain. It was hard work—my heart started to beat
faster, I began to perspire, and my legs felt wooden. I was not

doing this for fun (my idea of fun is more along the lines of doing jigsaw puzzles); I certainly was not doing it for the view—the mountains were shrouded in fog; I pressed on only because I knew the exercise was good for my health.

Then it happened. All of a sudden, my ascent took me above the fog and my efforts were rewarded with an incredible view of the towering Grand Tetons that had not been visible from below, due to the fog. It was as if those magnificent, snow-covered mountains had just burst forth out of the earth. For a moment I forgot my racing pulse and tired legs. The view at the top made it worth it all.

Proverbs 25:2 says, "It is the glory of God to conceal a matter; to search out a matter is the glory of kings." The fact that there are some things (many things!) that God knows that we don't is what makes Him God and us human. An essential part of God's glory and splendor is that He cannot be fully known by finite creatures. At the same time, *our* glory is to devote ourselves to searching out His ways, believing that one day our search will be rewarded.

Paul puts it another way. He reminds us that "now we see but a poor reflection as in a mirror. . . . Now I know in part." In other words, we know there is a stunning view out there; but from our current vantage point we can't see it—it is obscured by the fog of time and space. But Paul goes on to give us reason for great hope and anticipation: "*Then* we shall see face to face. . . . Then I shall know fully, even as I am fully known" (1 Corinthians 13:12, emphasis added). Yes, the pathway may be steep; hiking through Leviticus, 1 Chronicles, and Jude may seem strenuous and leave us with aching spiritual muscles.

But for those who press on to know Him, we have God's promise that one day we will step out of the fog into brilliant, clear, dazzling sunlight. The view at the top will be spectacular, for that is where at long last "we shall behold Him"—Jesus Himself—"face to face, in all of His glory."[7] And that's one view that will be well worth the wait!

MAKING IT PERSONAL

1. Record several specific blessings you have received from reading (or hearing) God's Word.

2. The Word of God is to the soul what food is to the body. Based on your intake of the Word over the past thirty days, how well-nourished are you spiritually?

3. Evaluate your current approach to reading the Scripture.

   - Do you read prayerfully? Are you conscious of your dependence on the Holy Spirit to give you understanding? Do you read the Word with the expressed intent to obey whatever God shows you?
   - Do you read thoughtfully? Do you take time to meditate on the meaning of what you are reading? Are you memorizing Scripture on a regular basis?
   - Do you read systematically? Are you getting a balanced spiritual diet by "partaking" from every portion of God's Word? Do you have a systematic plan for reading the Bible, to help you avoid overlooking certain portions? What is that plan?

4. If you don't already have a plan for regular Bible reading, ask the Lord to direct you as to where and how to start. Record the approach He puts on your heart.

   When will you set aside time in the next twenty-four hours to begin reading?

5. If you are already in the habit of reading Scripture, are you just going through an intellectual exercise (as the Pharisees did), or are you really getting to know Jesus through His Word?

▫▫▫ FROM THE HEART OF ▫▫▫
Jeannie Elliff

After my salvation in 1971, the Word that I had long struggled giving my attention to came alive for me! My quiet time is where I receive answers to questions, direction for my life, comfort, encouragement, conviction of sin, and cleansing of my heart.

The most important ingredient of my quiet time is the Word. I desperately need to hear what God has to say to me. Each day I face different issues; it is imperative that I get God's wisdom daily—*before* I am tempted to respond with the world's way of handling problems.

So early in the morning (no phone calls or interruptions this way), I go to my kitchen table, fix myself a cup of coffee or tea, and begin reading my Bible. This year I am reading straight through the *Women's Study Bible* (including all the study notes).

In the past, I've tried different, complicated systems of reading the Bible. I always seem to go back to the "ribbon approach"—turn to the ribbon, read several chapters, replace the ribbon. My life has always been pretty hectic; this is simple and works for me.

Worship is a natural outflowing of reading the Word. As I read, I see attributes of God and blessings and begin to worship and praise Him.

Over a period of years, I've developed my own personal prayer notebook. I keep it in my planner so it's with me everywhere I go. I have topics, people, and issues divided up for each day of the week.

Often, I will use various books for further study time later in the day, but I only use God's Word and my prayer notebook for my quiet time.

It is a blessed privilege to meet with my Lord every morning. I finished Genesis a few days ago and found myself weeping that it was over. How good our Lord is to give us such "wonderful words of life"!

Jeannie Elliff's husband, Tom, is a pastor in Del City, Oklahoma. They have served the Lord together through five pastorates, spanning thirty-three years, in addition to two years as missionaries in Zimbabwe. Jeannie is the mother of four children, all of whom are actively serving the Lord, and has thirteen grandchildren.

NOTES

1. William Gurnall, *Gleanings from William Gurnall*, comp. Hamilton Smith (Morgan, Pa.: Soli Deo Gloria, 1996), 106–7.
2. Thomas Watson, *Gleanings from Thomas Watson*, comp. Hamilton Smith (Morgan, Pa.: Soli Deo Gloria, 1995), 106, 112.
3. Donald S. Whitney, *Spiritual Disciplines for the Christian Life* (Colorado Springs: Navpress, 1991), 38.
4. Darlene Deibler Rose, *Evidence Not Seen* (San Francisco: Harper & Row, 1988), 143.
5. Richard Cecil, *The Remains of the Rev. Richard Cecil*, from the 11th London ed.; ed. Josiah Pratt (New York: Robert Carter; Philadelphia: Thomas Carter, 1843), 159.
6. Walk Thru the Bible Ministries; 4201 N. Peachtree Road, Atlanta, GA, 30341; 770/458-9300.
7. "We Shall Behold Him," by Dottie Rambo. Copyright 1977 John T. Benson Publishing Co./ ASCAP. All rights reserved. Used by permission of Brentwood-Benson Music Publishing, Inc.

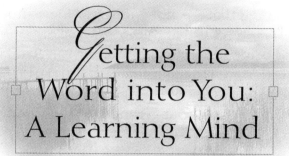

CHAPTER 9

Getting the Word into You: A Learning Mind

Have you ever had the experience of reading a portion of Scripture—perhaps even several pages or chapters—only to stop and realize that you have absolutely no idea what you just read? That has happened to me more times than I care to admit.

Or perhaps you find it difficult to concentrate when you are reading the Word. Your eyes may be reading words about the children of Israel in the wilderness or Jesus and His disciples in a boat; but your mind is thinking about the phone call you just received from your mother-in-law, your annual performance review scheduled for this afternoon, your daughter who is spending the weekend with her alcoholic father and his girlfriend—or a thousand other things that have nothing to do with what you are reading.

We have talked about the value and necessity of reading God's Word. That is the starting place in getting to know God. As C. H. Spurgeon said, "If you wish to know God, you must know His Word." Now I want to suggest a practical step that will help make the Word come alive within you. This practice will help you concentrate on what you are reading and can keep your devotions from becoming boring or dry.

In fact, as you incorporate this process into your walk with God, your quiet time may well become the time of day that you most look forward to. In time, you will find that you truly don't want to miss a single day of spending time in the Word.

Keep in mind that it is not enough that we should just *read* the Word. The object is that the words that are printed on the page would become indelibly written on our hearts. God never intended that we should merely get into His Word—His intent is that the Word should get into us.

So how do we go about getting the Word grafted into our hearts and lives? Here is one key.

 ## Write as You Read!

Without question, next to the Holy Spirit, the single greatest help in my personal devotional life has been to read the Scripture with paper and pen in hand, so I can record insights from the Word. As I write down what God is saying to my heart through His Word, the words are lifted off the page and become full of meaning and life to me.

The exciting thing is that this process does not have to be difficult or complex and does not require a graduate degree in theology. In fact, over the years I have challenged a number of young people to read through the Bible and write down two sentences about every chapter: one sentence summarizing the chapter and the other sentence expressing how that chapter spoke to them personally. Even this simple approach can be enormously beneficial.

There are several different types of writing that can be helpful in studying the Word; most of these are illustrated in the Scripture itself. As we proceed, I will share a number of examples of how I have incorporated these tools in my own devotional life. The point is not for you to imitate what I have done, but simply to give you some ideas to get you started on your own journey.

(By the way, don't let yourself get hung up in the mechanics. The particular Bible reading and study methods that are most helpful to someone else may not be as useful to you. The important thing is to make sure that you are getting into the Word and that the Word is getting into you. Find out which methods work best for you, and use them.)

1. WRITE OUT PORTIONS OF THE WORD

Prior to the invention of the printing press, people did not have their own copies of the Word of God. The Bible was painstakingly copied out by hand and passed on from one generation to the next.

I believe something precious may have been lost for those of us who can so easily purchase a printed version of the Word of God, and that there is value in taking time to copy out portions of the Scripture word for word. On several occasions in the Old Testament God instructed people to do this very thing.

When Moses went up on the mount to meet with God, the Lord said to him, "'Write down these words. . . .' And he wrote on the tablets the words of the covenant—the Ten Commandments" (Exodus 34:27–28).

Forty years later, as the children of Israel were preparing to enter the Promised Land, Moses rehearsed God's laws for the entire congregation and then instructed them: "Write them on the doorframes of your houses and on your gates" (Deuteronomy 6:9). (This verse has motivated me to display framed pictures with Scripture throughout my house. Those pieces serve as wonderful visual reminders of the ways of God, as well as ministering to others who visit in my home.)

Shortly before his death, Moses once again called the Israelites together and told them that after they crossed the Jordan River and entered Canaan they were to select some large stones, set them up on Mount Ebal (about thirty-five miles north of Jerusalem), and "write very clearly all the words of this law on these stones you have set up" (Deuteronomy 27:8).

Earlier we saw the instruction God gave to the kings of Israel:

> *When he takes the throne of his kingdom, he is to write for himself on a scroll a copy of this law. . . . It is to be with him, and he is to read it all the days of his life.* (DEUTERONOMY 17:18–19)

What was the point of this exercise? Do you remember in elementary school when the teacher would instruct the class to copy a list from the chalkboard or a page out of a textbook? It seemed like meaningless busywork at the time. But the teacher knew that if you wrote out the material for yourself, you were more likely to grasp and remember the concepts.

God knew how prone His people were to forget what He had told them. Over and over, He challenged them to "remember" Him, to remember His law, to remember what He had done for them. Writing out the Word of God was one practical way to help them remember.

And it can help us remember. Taking time to write out specific passages from the Word forces us to think about what we are reading and to observe the details of the text more carefully.

This afternoon I received a call from a friend who shared the blessing he has been receiving from copying out the gospel of Luke. One of my staff has set a goal to write out the entire Bible by hand. Another friend copies paragraphs of the Bible onto three-by-five-inch cards and then memorizes and meditates on those passages each morning while running on the treadmill.

2. WRITE IN YOUR BIBLE

This suggestion is not specifically found in the Scripture (remember that hardly anyone owned a copy of the Bible before the sixteenth century), but it has been a practical help and blessing in my growing love affair with the Word. When I was a child, my parents encouraged us to underline verses that we found especially meaningful. (At one point, I got carried away with the idea, leading my father to suggest that perhaps I should underline only those verses that were *not* particularly meaningful to me!)

Over the years, I have read and "marked up" many different copies of the Bible. Each of those Bibles tells a story of my personal journey of faith during a specific period of time. In addition to underlining phrases or verses for emphasis, I frequently circle or bracket repeated words or phrases. I also write cross references in the margin (more about these last two points in a few moments), as well as jot down notes about the meaning of specific words or phrases in the passage.

When the Lord uses a verse or passage to address a specific need in my life or to encourage or convict my heart in an unusual way, I often indicate the date (and sometimes the city) on which that personal encounter with the living God took place. The space in the margins is sometimes used to write brief, personal responses to the truth, such as, "Yes, Lord," "I agree," "Change my heart, O God," or "Make this true in my life, Lord."

3. RECORD INSIGHTS INTO THE WORD OF GOD

When the apostle John was in exile on the isle of Patmos, he was given a vision of heaven. The Lord Jesus appeared to him and said, "Write on a scroll what you see. . . . Write, therefore, what you have seen" (Revelation 1:11, 19).

Over the years, I have recorded in my personal journals hundreds and hundreds of pages of observations and insights that the Holy Spirit has shown me while reading and meditating on the Word. Capturing these insights helps us to clarify, understand, and remember the ways of God. The process of writing them down deepens our love and appreciation for the truth of God's Word.

You say, How do I know what to write? Many Bible teachers suggest asking three basic questions each time you read the Bible:

- What does it say? (Make observations about the text.)
- What does it mean? (Look for the implications or the interpretation of the text.)
- What should I do? (Make practical application of the text.)

Each time I write in my devotional journal, I record the date and the passage I am reading. I then proceed to answer those questions.

Under this point ("Record Insights into the Word of God"), we will consider some practical ways to go about answering the first two of those questions: *What does it say?* and *What does it mean?* We will look at the third question, *What should I do?*, under the next main point ("Record Your Responses to the Word of God").

What does it say? (Observation)

How can we learn what the passage says and understand what it means? Martin Luther explained how he went about this process:

> I study my Bible as I gather apples. First, I shake the whole tree that the ripest may fall. Than I shake each limb, and when I have shaken each limb I shake each branch and every twig. Then I look under every leaf.

Luther was suggesting that we should start with the most obvious, simple observations about the text, and then probe more deeply for further understanding.

The following exercises will help you make observations about what the Scripture is actually saying. You probably will not want to use all of these exercises for every passage you read, but these are things to keep in mind as you record your observations:

1. *Summarize.* After reading the passage, try to come up with a title for the entire book, the chapter, and the individual

paragraphs. Look for a key verse that captures the heart of the passage. Write a brief summary overview of the passage, including the major points.

2. *Paraphrase.* Try to write the passage in your own words.
3. *Ask questions.* Use the same questions you would ask if you were writing a newspaper account:

- *Who* wrote it? said it? about whom? speaking to whom?
- *What* happened? What are the main events? the major ideas? the theme?
- *When* was it written? Did the events take place? Will it yet happen?
- *Where* did this happen? Will it yet happen?
- *Why* was this written? (Sometimes the answer will be right in the text, as in John 20:31 and 1 John 5:13.) Did he say that? Did he go there?
- *How* did it happen? Is it done?

Write down any additional questions that the passage raises in your mind. You may not be able to come up with the answers right away, but frequently you will find that other passages will provide the answers you are looking for.

4. *Look for patterns.* Look for repeated words or phrases to help you understand what the author intends to emphasize. For example:

- As you read the book of Leviticus, circle the words *holy, clean, unclean,* and related words every time they appear. Then summarize what this book teaches about holiness.
- In the book of 1 John, highlight the repeated phrase *this is how we know,* to help you make a list of evidences of genuine salvation.

- In 1 Peter, mark every reference to *suffering* and *glory* to see the connection between the two. *Submission* is another recurring theme in 1 Peter. Make a note of each relationship where someone is to be submissive.

- In Ezekiel, the phrase *that they will know that I am the* LORD appears nearly sixty times in forty-eight chapters. What does that tell you about God's purposes in our world?

- In the book of Hebrews, Jesus is said to be "superior to the angels (1:4) and to Moses (3:3), and His ministry is said to be superior to that of the Old Testament priests (8:6).

5. *Look for cross-references.* As you become more familiar with the Bible, you will find that as you read a passage, the Holy Spirit will bring to mind other verses that relate to, confirm, or shed further light on what you are reading.

For example, this morning I read the fifth chapter of Daniel, where Daniel refused to accept the payment that King Belshazzar offered him for interpreting the writing on the wall. Immediately I thought of two other passages I read recently where godly men did the same thing (Elisha—2 Kings 5:16; Abraham—Genesis 14:21–24). In the margin next to Daniel 5:17, I jotted down these cross-references. God used these passages to caution me about the danger of ministering for personal or material gain.

There are several tools you will find extremely helpful as you seek to discover what a passage is saying.

An English dictionary is useful for looking up the basic meaning of words. If you really want a blessing, purchase Daniel Webster's original *1828 Dictionary*, which gives rich, biblical definitions of many English words such as grace, faith, repentance, and blessing.[1]

Various translations and even paraphrases of the Bible can shed fresh light on passages and help in understanding their meaning.[2]

Strong's Exhaustive Concordance is helpful for doing word studies and discovering which word in the original language is being translated in the English Bible (King James Version). If you are not familiar with the Hebrew and Greek dictionaries at the back of *Strong's*, ask your pastor or another experienced student of the Word to show you how to use them. If you are using the *New International Version* as your basic study Bible, you will find helpful *The NIV Exhaustive Concordance*, ed. Edward W. Goodrick and John R. Kohlenberger III (Grand Rapids: Zondervan, 1990). Similarly, the *New American Standard Exhaustive Concordance*, ed. Robert L. Thomas (Nashville: Holman, 1981), will be useful to persons using the NASB.

Vine's Expository Dictionary of New Testament Words is a wonderful tool to help you understand the meaning and usage of specific words in the English Bible.

Commentaries and study Bibles can be helpful in understanding difficult passages or gaining background on such things as biblical authors, locations, characters, and customs.[3] However, try to refer to commentaries only after you have done your own reading, meditation, and study of the passage. God has given you His Holy Spirit to help you understand His Word. Commentaries and study Bible notes are not divinely inspired; they are merely the work of men who have sought to understand and explain the Word.

What does it mean? (Implications/Interpretation)

In addition to the questions you have asked to help determine what the passage says, as you read the Bible ask these kinds of questions to help you understand the implications of the text:

1. What does this passage teach me about God?
2. What does this passage teach me about Jesus?
3. What does this passage teach me about man?
4. Are there any promises to claim?
5. Are there any commands to obey?

6. Are there any examples to follow?

7. Are there any sins to avoid?

4. RECORD YOUR RESPONSES TO THE WORD OF GOD

What should I do? (Application)

Some time ago, I listened to several audiotape messages by a pastor who is a gifted expositor of the Word. He began each message by opening up a specific text of Scripture and explaining what it says and what it means. Then he came to a certain point in each message where he made the same statement: "That's the *'what.'* Now, the question is: *'So what?'*" This pastor isn't satisfied for his people just to know *what* the passage says, as important as that is; he wants to be sure they also make practical application of the truth to their lives.

God told Ezekiel that the problem with His people was that "[they] sit before you to listen to your words, but they do not put them into practice" (Ezekiel 33:31).

Hebrews 4:2 tells us that "the message [the children of Israel] heard was of no value to them, because those who heard did not combine it with faith"—that is, they didn't act on what they heard.

James makes the same point: "Do not merely listen to the word, and so deceive yourselves. *Do what it says*" (James 1:22, emphasis added).

The old-time evangelist Gipsy Smith said, "What makes the difference is not how many times you have been through the Bible, but how many times and how thoroughly the Bible has been through you."

As you meditate on the Scripture, ask such questions as:

- How does this truth apply to my life? to my situation?

- In view of this truth, what changes need to be made in my life?

- What practical steps can I take to apply this truth to my life?

Everything we read in God's Word calls for some type of response. That response may be to

- exercise faith in God's promises or character;
- humble ourselves and acknowledge our need;
- confess our sins;
- turn from our old ways of thinking;
- obey some command we have been neglecting;
- worship and adore the God who has revealed Himself;
- forgive one who has wronged us;
- seek forgiveness from someone we have wronged;
- seek to reconcile a broken relationship;
- give to meet the need of another;
- share the good news of Jesus Christ with a non-Christian friend or relative; or
- cry out to God on behalf of a needy friend.

(In chapters 10 and 11 we will consider how to respond to God's Word in praise and prayer.)

Recording the responses that the Spirit has led you to make will help move you past *hearing* the Word to *doing* it. You may want to write out your response in the form of a prayer expressing your commitment to the Lord. Another helpful step is to share with another believer what God has put on your heart and ask her to help hold you accountable to obey the Lord.

In the book of Nehemiah we read about a great revival that God sent to the exiles who had returned to Israel. The revival was birthed when the congregation gathered together to listen to Ezra the priest read the Word of God in a service that lasted most of the day, continued for another seven days, and then resumed two weeks later. (Can you imagine going to church and standing for hours at a time with no program other than to listen to the reading of the Word, followed by time to respond in worship and confession? We just might have another revival if we did that today!)

The ninth chapter of Nehemiah records a long prayer of corporate confession made by the repentant Israelites. The prayer concludes with these words: "In view of all this, we are making a binding agreement, *putting it in writing*" (v. 38, emphasis added). Chapter 10 records the details of the covenant they made that day. It includes promises to obey God in such matters as marriage, Sabbath observance, and tithing. By writing out and signing the covenant they became more accountable for their response to the Word they had heard.

My own journals include many such responses to the Word of God. Many of those responses are in the form of prayers—prayers of thanksgiving, praise, confession, repentance, intercession, or supplication.

For example, on one occasion, I recorded the following response to Jesus' teaching about forgiveness in Matthew 18:23–35:

> How often I am like that forgiven servant who refused to forgive, but demanded payment from his fellow servant who owed him a pittance.
>
> O Father, You have had compassion on me and loosed me from the infinite debt of sin. Yet sometimes I still insist on taking my fellow servants "by the throat," dealing roughly with them and insisting that they fulfill some relatively small obligation to me.
>
> Forgive me for not treating others with the same compassion I have received from You. May I be as generous in dispensing grace to others as You have been with me.

In the book of Joshua we read about an encounter between Joshua and a heavenly messenger (most likely a pre-incarnate manifestation of Christ). When Joshua looked up and saw the stranger standing before him with a drawn sword in his hand, Joshua approached him to find out whose side he was on. The warrior replied,

"As commander of the army of the LORD I have now come." Then Joshua fell facedown to the ground in reverence, and asked him, "What message does my Lord have for his servant?"

The commander of the LORD'S army replied, "Take off your sandals, for the place where you are standing is holy." And Joshua did so. (JOSHUA 5:14–15)

Notice the progression here: The Lord approached His servant. As soon as Joshua realized to whom he was speaking, he humbled himself and asked, "What do you want to say to me?" He listened carefully to the Lord's words and then immediately obeyed the voice of the Lord.

This issue of obedience to the Word of God is crucial in cultivating a close relationship with God, as reflected in the following prayer by C. H. Spurgeon:

Lord, may Thy Word be the supreme ruler of our being. May we give ourselves up to its sacred law to be obedient to its every hint, wishing in all things, even in the least, to do the will of God from the heart and having every thought brought into captivity to the mind of the Spirit of God.[4]

5. RECORD MILESTONES IN YOUR SPIRITUAL PILGRIMAGE

Shortly after the children of Israel were delivered out of Egypt, they were attacked by a fierce band of Amalekites. On the day of the battle, Joshua led the Israelite army out to face the enemy. This was Joshua's first battle, and God used the occasion to teach this eager young leader to rely, not on his natural strength or ability, but on the power of God.

When the battle was ready to begin down in the valley, Moses walked to the top of a nearby hill, grasped his shepherd's rod ("the rod of God") with both hands, and raised his hands up to heaven. What happened next is recorded for us in some detail in Exodus chapter 17:

As long as Moses held up his hands, the Israelites were winning, but whenever he lowered his hands, the Amalekites were winning. When Moses' hands grew tired, they took a stone and put it under him and he sat on it. Aaron and Hur held his hands up—one on one side, one on the other—so that his hands remained steady till sunset. So Joshua over-came the Amalekite army with the sword. (EXODUS 17:11–13)

End of battle. End of story. Not quite.

God did not want Joshua ever to forget that the Amalekites were His eternal enemies and that He alone had the power to overcome them. So the Lord said to Moses, "Write this on a scroll as something to be remembered" (Exodus 17:14). This is perhaps the first biblical illustration of what many today call "journaling."

You wouldn't think there was much chance of Joshua ever forgetting what had just taken place—much as when God moves in a significant way in our lives we think we will never forget what has happened. But God wanted to be sure that, even when Joshua was an old man with lots of victories un-der his belt, he would have a permanent record of this partic-ular battle—a written reminder of the true Source of his power.

That unusual battle wasn't the only time Moses made a "journal entry." Throughout the forty years of the wilderness wandering of the children of Israel, Moses kept a record of the LORD'S dealings with His people. Why? Because God told him to. "At the Lord's command Moses recorded the stages in their journey" (Numbers 33:2).

I think there were at least three reasons God told Moses to keep this journal: (1) so the *Israelites* would remember what they had learned of the heart and ways of God at each stage of the journey; (2) so their *children* might learn the same lessons; and (3) so *we*, too, could learn from their experiences.

In fact, the New Testament makes two specific references to Moses' journal: "For everything that was written in the past was written to teach us, so that through endurance and the encouragement of the Scriptures we might have hope" (Romans

15:4). "These things. . . were written down as warnings for us" (1 Corinthians 10:11).

Over the years I have kept a record of many significant markers in my walk with God. While most of these experiences center around specific circumstances in my life, invariably they are birthed out of the Word of God, as the Spirit uses whatever I may be reading at that time to shed light on my path. The following was written shortly after the death of a beloved spiritual mentor. It was a response to Psalm 146:

> The deepest needs of my life can not be met by any created being, but only by God Himself. He is fully able to meet every need, whether of the oppressed, the hungry, the prisoner, the blind, those that are bowed down, the strangers, the fatherless, or the widow (vv. 7–9).
>
> Those human instruments that I have looked to in the past for help have now died, as the Word says they will (vv. 3–4). They can no longer help me. So, Lord God, as one who is fatherless, hungry, bowed down, and needy, I look to You to meet my needs. "Happy is he that hath the God of Jacob for his help, whose hope is in the Lord his God" (v. 5 kjv). "Whom have I in heaven but thee? and there is none upon earth that I desire beside thee" (Psalm 73:25 KJV).

In the Old Testament, God instructed His people to observe specific feasts each year. Each of these feasts represented some aspect of God's redemptive plan. In fact, that is where the whole concept of "holidays" (that is, "holy days") originated. In my own life, I have tried to set aside time on special days (both my natural and spiritual birthdays, the beginning of a new year, and so on) to meditate on God's goodness and to seek His face for the coming year. One lengthy journal entry, a prayer written on my thirty-fifth birthday, reads in part:

> As I look ahead to another year of life, I am reminded that I may not spend another year here on this earth. Within that space, You may call me to heaven, or the Lord Jesus may return for His Bride. "Teach [me] to number [my] days and recognize

how few they are; help [me] to spend them as [I] should"
(Psalm 90:12 TLB).

Help me to live whatever days I have remaining in light of
eternity. I humbly seek Your blessing and Your favor, for having
them, I lack nothing. I would seek to please You rather than men.
This year I ask . . .

— to know and love You in ever-increasing intimacy
— for the protection of Your Spirit over my heart, my mind,
   and my affections
— that You would keep me from sin and from the Evil One
— to be faithful in fulfilling the ministry You have entrusted
   to me—faithful in small tasks as well as large, in secret and
   obscurity as well as in public
— for a heart full of love for others
— that You might make me fruitful
— that every day might be lived to the fullest and in the constant, conscious awareness of Your presence
— that I might walk in the light before You and others, without guile or pretense
— that I might be holy and humble before You and others

These things I ask in Jesus' Name, and for the sake of Your
Kingdom. May Your Kingdom come, and Your will be done here
on earth—and in this grateful heart—as it is in heaven. Amen.

One Woman's Testimony

A number of years ago I received the following testimony
from a woman who had attended a conference where I had
spoken the previous year. You can sense the great joy she experienced as she learned how to get into the Word and get the
Word into her life.

Last fall I attended a women's retreat where you taught the
entire book of the Song of Solomon. You paralleled the Bride and
the Bridegroom's relationship to our relationship with the Lord.
You pointed out that when the Bride first lost her Beloved she

wasn't willing to venture out from her bed to search for him (Song of Solomon 3:1). God showed me that this was true in my own life. I wasn't willing to journey into God's Word to seek Him, thus building a strong relationship with Him. Most of my growth had come because of someone else's hard work. If I needed help in a certain area, I would read a book, listen to a tape, or wait for a sermon on the subject.

I am not saying I never read my Bible, because I did. But reading my Bible and studying God's Word are not the same. I was unbalanced. The following analogy helped me understand the difference.

I love to shop in those aroma-filled grocery stores. Fresh bread is baked in ovens. Wonderful smells lure you to the bakery counter, and you can't resist. At dinner that evening you pass real butter and fresh bread. Everyone goes, "Mmmmmm!" Did you enjoy that bread? I sure did. Did you do the work of preparing it? Was it wrong to enjoy it because you didn't do the work? No!

Now consider this scene. Again you are at the store, only this time you buy flour, yeast, eggs, butter, and milk. At home you pull out a large bowl, measuring utensils, a few pans, your ingredients, and a cookbook. Now you start your own aromas drifting. Your home, not the store, smells wonderful. You are filled with a sense of satisfaction as you set the beautiful loaf of golden brown bread on the table. Your family says, "Wow! Did you make that?" Which bread did you enjoy more? Digging a truth from God's Word, on your own, gives you a real sense of accomplishment, just as making fresh bread would.

When I left the retreat I knew what change had to take place in my life. I would have to begin a consistent study of God's Word. How was I to accomplish this, since I had depended on others for so long? Trusting God to show me, I prayed and asked the Lord what to study.

Presently I am doing word studies. These have caused real growth in my life. One morning I used a Strong's Concordance and a Thompson Chain Reference Bible to study the word "revenge." Using these tools, I traced the word "revenge" through Scripture. I learned much about revenge and words of a similar nature, such as "vengeance" in Romans 12:19.

When I went outside that morning, I discovered that someone had pelted our newly painted tan garage with ripe cherries. Then they walked around the house and let the freshly primed windows have it. What surprised me more than the cherries was my reaction. Soap and water in hand, I began to wash it off. I did-n't even get angry. What a victory to learn we aren't to desire re-venge and then see it worked out in my own life.

That was a dramatic example of what I have learned. Every day doesn't bring forth such powerful results. But as I reflect on the past year, I realize the groping is gone. I am a stronger Christian because of studying God's Word for myself.

"*I* Saw with My Own Eyes"

Three thousand years ago, an Arabian queen learned of a foreign king whose achievements and wisdom were legendary. Determined to see for herself, she gathered together a large caravan carrying rare and expensive gifts and then traveled twelve hundred miles to meet the monarch. Upon her arrival, she was warmly welcomed by the king. He listened as she told him all that was on her mind and asked many difficult questions. Her questions were no match for him—he answered them willingly and easily. When she saw the vast wealth and wisdom of the king, the Queen of Sheba was overcome.

> *She said to the king, "The report I heard in my own country about your achievements and your wisdom is true. But I did not believe these things* until I came and saw with my own eyes. *Indeed, not even half was told me; in wisdom and wealth you have far exceeded the report I heard. How happy your men must be! How happy your officials, who continually stand before you and hear your wisdom!"* (1 KINGS 10:6–8, emphasis added)

When the queen finally left to return to her homeland, she did not go away empty-handed:

> *King Solomon gave [her] all she desired and asked for; he gave her more than she had brought to him.* (2 CHRONICLES 9:12)

My friend, it is one thing to listen to others speak of the

wonders of King Jesus. It is quite another thing to make the effort to go and meet Him for yourself—to see firsthand His vast stores of wealth, to ask Him your hard questions, to share all that is on your heart, and to listen intently as He shares with you the secrets of His kingdom. When you have met Him in this way, you will understand why His servants consider it their highest joy to stand before Him each day and hear His wisdom.

And when you go back to your place—your home, your job, your neighborhood—you will not go empty-handed. You will return with more than your hands and heart can contain. For He will give you all the desires of your heart—far more than you ever could have brought to Him.

Have you been relying on secondhand reports about the greatness of God? Why not *"taste and see [for yourself] that the LORD is good"* (PSALM 34:8).

MAKING IT PERSONAL

Note: The "Making It Personal" section for this chapter is longer than usual. It has been designed to help you put into practice what you have learned in this chapter by guiding you through the study of a specific passage from God's Word. You may want to set aside one or two extended blocks of time in your schedule over the next several days in order to get the most out of this section.

1. Read Psalm 19. Ask God to speak to you through this familiar passage and to make it fresh to your heart.

    a. In your journal (any kind of notebook with lined pages will do), write out the entire psalm, word for word.

    b. Record *observations* about this passage ("What does it *say?*"), using some or all of the following suggestions:

    • *Summarize.* What title would you give to this chapter? Divide the chapter into two or more paragraphs and suggest a title for each. Write a one-paragraph summary or overview of the passage.

    • *Paraphrase.* Write out this passage in your own words.

    • *Ask questions.* Who wrote this psalm? Why did he write it? What is the connection between "the heavens" (vv. 1–6) and "the law of the LORD" (vv. 7–11)? How are they alike? What synonyms are used in this passage for the Word of God? What adjectives does the author use to describe the Word of God? What benefits and blessings does the Word bring to our lives? What two kinds of sins does the author pray to be delivered from (vv. 12–13)? What does the psalmist want the Word of God to accomplish in his life?

    • *Look for patterns.* What pattern do you see in the four parallel lines of vv. 7–8?

    • *Look for cross-references.* Using a concordance, the references in the margin of your Bible, or your memory, list four Scripture references that relate to specific phrases in Psalm 19. (For example, relate Proverbs 8:19 to Psalm 19:10.)

- *Use study tools.* Select a word or phrase from Psalm 19 that you would like to understand better. Use one of the tools recommended in this chapter (English dictionary; alternate translation; *Strong's Exhaustive Concordance, The NIV Exhaustive Concordance,* or the *New American Standard Exhaustive Concordance*) to gain further insight on that word or phrase.

c. Record some of the *implications* of this passage ("What does it mean?"). Consider the following types of questions:

- Why is the Word of God so vital and valuable to the child of God?
- What are some consequences we may experience if the Word of God is not kept central in our daily lives?
- Why does the Word of God not produce the desired results in the life of every believer?
- God promises "great reward" to those who "keep" His Word (v. 11). What does it mean to "keep" His Word?
- How does the Word of God help protect us from sin?

d. Record specific, practical *applications* that the Holy Spirit helps you make from this passage. Seek to engraft this passage into your life, using some or all of the following suggestions:

- Which of the benefits and blessings in verses 7–11 would you like to experience in a greater measure? The Word of God is designed to accomplish these results in our lives. What practical steps can you take to make the Word a higher priority in your life?
- Are you aware of anything in the Word of God that you are not currently obeying? What do you need to do to repent of going your own way and to begin walking in obedience to His Word?
- Pray aloud the prayer of the psalmist in verses 12–13. Then express the same prayer in your own words.
- Select one key verse from this psalm; memorize that verse and meditate on it over the next twenty-four hours.
- Write a prayer expressing to God your desire to feast on His Word and to have it engrafted into your life.

- Share with a friend or family member what God has said to you through this passage. Ask that individual to hold you accountable for any specific steps of action the Lord has laid on your heart.

2. Choose one of the following exercises to record milestones in your spiritual pilgrimage:

   a. Who are the individuals who have had the greatest influence on your walk with God? How have they impacted your life?

   b. Record the spiritual highlights of the past year. What major events or circumstances have you walked through? What have you learned from each about the heart and ways of God?

   c. Choose three or four attributes of God and record a specific instance in your life in which God has demonstrated each of those qualities.

   d. Write a three- to five-page "spiritual autobiography," summarizing how you came to faith in Christ and highlighting key stages of your spiritual pilgrimage and growth.

Tex Tippit

We become like the people with whom we spend time. My heart's desire is to reflect Jesus. That is why I choose to spend time with Him. I want to know Him more intimately, thus enabling me to make Him known more effectively.

As I face various obstacles, I claim related Scriptures. When I am tired, I claim the promise of Psalm 3:5 that He will give the sleep I need. When my schedule is busy, I claim Ephesians 5:15–16 and ask Him to guide my schedule. Psalm 119:18 is a helpful prayer when the Word seems "dry," or when I start to skim over a familiar passage. When my thoughts wander, I claim 2 Corinthians 10:3–5 and ask Him to bring every thought into captivity to Christ.

In addition to reading passages that lead me to praise the Lord, I read the Word systematically for an overall view. I read the Scripture as God's personal "love letter" to me. In order to see clearly what God is saying to me and how to apply His truth to my life, I find it helpful to put on my "spiritual eyeglasses," or what I call my "specs." As I read, I look for

> **S**in to forsake
> **P**romises to claim
> **E**xamples to follow
> **C**ommands to obey
> **S**tumbling blocks/errors to avoid

Consistent journaling helps clarify my thoughts, holds me accountable, and encourages me as I am reminded of His answers to specific requests.

Praying aloud helps focus my thoughts. My husband defines prayer as the "communication of two hearts." I try not only to talk to the Lord, but to listen as He speaks to me.

Tex Tippit is the wife of author and international evangelist Sammy Tippit, and the mother of two grown children. Tex is actively involved in a citywide women's prayer ministry in San Antonio, Texas, and has ministered with her husband in many different countries around the world.

NOTES

1. Webster's *1828 Dictionary* may be ordered from the Foundation for American Christian Education (F.A.C.E.), P.O. Box 9444, Chesapeake, VA 23321–9444.

2. Excellent translations include the King James Version, the *New King James Version*, the *New American Standard Bible*, and the *New International Version*. Popular paraphrases and translations are *The Living Bible*, *The New Living Translation*, and *The Amplified Bible*. Another useful resource for comparing translations of specific phrases is *The New Testament from 26 Translations* (Zondervan).

3. Some of the commentaries and study Bibles I have found helpful: *The NIV Study Bible* (Zondervan); *The MacArthur Study Bible* (Word); *The Bible Knowledge Commentary*, ed. John F. Walvoord and Roy B. Zuck (Victor Books); *The Wycliffe Bible Commentary*, ed. Charles F. Pfeiffer and Everett F. Harrison (Moody).

4. C. H. Spurgeon, *C. H. Spurgeon's Prayers*, with an Introduction by Dinsdale T. Young (Grand Rapids: Baker, 1978), 125.

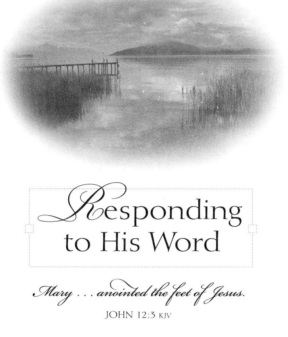

$\mathscr{R}$esponding to His Word

Mary ... anointed the feet of Jesus.

JOHN 12:3 KJV

$\mathscr{A}$fter a very few minutes my soul has been led to confession, or to thanksgiving, or to intercession, or to supplication. . . . When thus I have been for a while making confession or intercession or supplication, or have given thanks, I go on to the next words or verse, turning all, as I go on, into prayer for myself or others, as the Word may lead to it. . . .

The result of this is that there is always a good deal of confession, thanksgiving, supplication, or intercession mingled with my meditation, and that my inner man invariably is even sensibly nourished and strengthened, and that by breakfast time, with rare exceptions, I am in a peaceful if not happy state of heart.

GEORGE MÜLLER

CHAPTER 10

The Perfume of Praise: A Loving Heart

"He is aliiiiive! He is aliiiiive!" It was Easter Sunday morning. My five-year-old nephew was to be baptized that day. "Nana" had flown into town to share in the occasion. As the family was getting ready for church, she heard little "Mookie's" unmistakable voice coming from the bathroom down the hall. She quietly slipped into the hallway to see what was happening. There stood the child, on a step stool in front of the mirror, carefully combing his hair, then straightening his shirt and pants, while singing at the top of his lungs, totally oblivious to anyone who might be listening in as he joyously serenaded the Lord.

Children sometimes have a way of grasping things that grown-ups miss.

Take the time that children shouted out praises to Jesus in the temple. It was the week before the Passover. The temple was busy with people making last-minute purchases. Incensed by the corruption and crass commercialism taking place in what was intended to be a house of worship and prayer, Jesus had just made quite a scene by driving the money changers and merchants from the outer court of the temple. Now He was attracting attention by healing the blind and the lame—outcasts who normally were not even allowed in the temple. To make matters worse, the children who had seen it all were loudly acclaiming Him as the Messiah—"Hosanna to the Son of David!" they cried out.

That did it. Those religious leaders had had more than they could take. Matthew tells us that when they "saw the wonderful things he did and the children shouting in the temple area, . . . they were indignant. 'Do you hear what these children are saying?' they asked him" (Matthew 21:15–16). The implication: "Make them stop!"

Get the picture? The chief priests and teachers of the law were the ones who were supposed to be experts in worship. But instead of encouraging the people to worship God, they were busy running a lucrative business. When Jesus had compassion on the sick and demonstrated His power by healing them, and when the children responded in simple, heartfelt worship, those same leaders got upset and moved in to put a stop to the whole thing.

When the children saw the wonderful things Jesus did, they worshiped (which is what you were supposed to do in the temple!). When the temple leaders saw the wonderful things Jesus did, they worried about the religious and political implications of this movement. What if this man, lauded by the people as King, toppled their centuries-old religious system? And what if the whole commotion antagonized the local Roman authorities?

The children shouted out their praises without inhibition, while the leaders feared that things might get out of control—their control, that is. The children were preoccupied with Jesus—they were not the least bit conscious of how others saw them or what anyone else was thinking. The leaders, on the other hand, were concerned about how they looked, about holding on to their position, about what everyone else would think about this whole scene.

This time the children had it right. The grown-ups had it wrong.

RESPONDING TO GOD

We have considered the necessity and delight of getting into the Word of God and getting His Word into us. We have shown that it is through the Word that we come to know God—His heart, His ways, His character, His eternal purposes and plan. Now we turn our attention to responding to what God reveals to us in His Word.

God desires to establish two-way communication with us, much as we long for two-way communication with our family and friends. When you call a close friend to share a piece of exciting news, you expect her to respond, to share in your enthusiasm. When you express your love to your husband, you want to know that he has heard you and to be reassured of his love for you. When you present a much-anticipated gift to one of your children, you are delighted to hear, "Thanks, Mom!"

As our loving, heavenly Father, God wants to speak to us—which requires that we learn to be still and listen to His Word. But He also wants us to respond to what He has said. Praise (or worship) and prayer are two of the most basic responses to God. We will consider the first of those responses in this chapter; in the next chapter, we will turn to the matter of prayer.

This two-way process of listening and responding to God is illustrated in the life of a woman who was one of Jesus' dearest friends. In chapter 2 we saw Mary of Bethany sitting at the feet of Jesus and listening to His Word (Luke 10:38–42). But Mary was not satisfied just to *receive* from Jesus. As she listened to His heart, she longed to *respond* to Him—to give back to Him, as He had given to her. Three of the Gospels record Mary's poignant display of devotion as she anointed Jesus' head and feet at a dinner prepared in His honor (Matthew 26:6–13; Mark 14:3–9; John 12:1–8).

Mary had lingered in Jesus' presence, she had listened to His words, she had learned from His life, and she had experienced His unconditional love for her. Worship was the natural response of her grateful heart. And so it should be with us. Here's the point: *Whenever God reveals Himself or displays His power and love, a response is called for.*

Exodus 14 gives us the dramatic account of God's parting the waters of the Red Sea so that His people might be delivered from the Egyptian army. What was the response of the Israelites to this great display of God's redemptive power?

> *Then Moses and the Israelites sang this song to the LORD:*
> *"I will sing to the LORD,*
> *for he is highly exalted.*
> *The horse and its rider*
> *he has hurled into the sea.*
> *The LORD is my strength and my song;*
> *he has become my salvation.*
> *He is my God, and I will praise him,*
> *my father's God, and I will exalt him."*
>
> —EXODUS 15:1–2

When the crippled beggar outside the temple saw the power of God revealed on his behalf, he responded by "walking and jumping, and praising God" (Acts 3:8).

When Jesus revealed His power and grace by cleansing ten desperate lepers, "one of them, when he saw he was healed, came back, praising God in a loud voice. He threw himself at Jesus' feet and thanked him" (Luke 17:15–16). The fact that nine of the ten failed to return to give thanks did not go unnoticed by Jesus. Jesus asked, "'Was no one found to return and give praise to God except this foreigner?'" (v. 18).

As you look back on all that God has done for you, how adequately do you feel you have expressed your gratitude and praise to Him?

WHAT IS WORSHIP?

Worship is a believer's response to God's revelation of Himself. It is expressing wonder, awe, and gratitude for the worthiness, the greatness, and the goodness of our Lord. It is the appropriate response to God's person, His provision, His power, His promises, and His plan.

Praise and thanksgiving are two important dimensions of worship. Praise is verbal or visible adoration of God—for who He is. Thanksgiving involves expressing gratitude for what He has done. Praise focuses on the Giver, while thanksgiving acknowledges His gifts.

Inasmuch as the Scripture does not make a strong distinction between praise, worship, and thanksgiving, they can all be considered one appropriate response to what we have come to know of God through His Word.

Why Praise?

We should praise the Lord because *God loves praise and He seeks worshipers* (John 4:23). Praise is important to God; every time you praise Him, you are fulfilling one of the deepest desires of His heart.

We should praise the Lord because *praise is the primary, eternal occupation of heaven.* In Revelation 4–5, God gives the apostle John a vision of the throne room of heaven. In that vision, John sees more than 100 million angels (5:11) who have one full-time responsibility, day and night: to worship the One who sits on that throne and the Lamb who is at His right hand (4:6–8; 5:12). The saints and citizens of heaven who have gone before us are there as well, praising and worshiping the Lord. In a sense, when we praise the Lord here on earth, we are having a "dress rehearsal" for what we will spend an eternity doing in heaven. How much "practice" are you getting in preparation for that eternal concert of praise in heaven?

We should praise the Lord because *He commands us to praise Him*. Did you know that the most frequently repeated command in all of God's Word is the command to "praise the Lord"? (I suspect it may also be the most frequently neglected command.)

We should praise the Lord because *He deserves our worship and praise*. He alone is worthy "to receive glory and honor and power" (Revelation 4:11). He is the God above all gods, the King above all kings, the Lord above all lords. There is no one like Him in heaven or on earth. He is worthy of all the praise we could ever lavish on Him.

We should praise the Lord because *we were made to bring Him pleasure*, and praise pleases Him. Do you ever wonder what your purpose is here on this earth? When you praise God, you are fulfilling the highest purpose for which He created you.

We should praise the Lord because *praise takes us into His presence and brings down His glory*. Psalm 22:3 (KJV) tells us that God actually inhabits the praises of His people. As one preacher put it, "Praise is God's address." The psalmist invites us to "enter his gates with thanksgiving and his courts with praise" (Psalm 100:4).

At the dedication of Solomon's temple, a massive choir, accompanied by 120 trumpeters, as well as other instruments, "raised their voices in praise to the LORD and sang: 'He is good; his love endures forever'" (2 Chronicles 5:13). At that moment, "the glory of the LORD filled the temple of God" (v. 14).

Do you want to see the glory of God? Do you want to be close to Him? Through praise you may go right up to His throne and into the place of His most intimate presence.

We should praise the Lord because *praise is a cure for spiritual dryness*. God has created us in such a way that we are thirsty for Him. When we look to things and people on this earth to satisfy our thirst, we become dry and discontent. But when we lift our eyes up to Him in praise, our hearts are filled. One day when David was hiding out from King Saul in the wilderness of Judah, feeling dry and needy, he discovered this powerful secret:

O God, you are my God,
    earnestly I seek you;
my soul thirsts for you,
    my body longs for you,
in a dry and weary land
    where there is no water.

I have seen you in the sanctuary
    and beheld your power and your glory.
Because your love is better than life,
    my lips will glorify you.
I will praise you as long as I live,
    and in your name I will lift up my hands.
My soul will be satisfied as with the richest of foods;
    with singing lips my mouth will praise you.

—PSALM 63:1–5

Are you spiritually dry and thirsty? Begin to praise the Lord and He will fill you with Himself until your thirst is quenched and your cup overflows.

We should praise the Lord because *praise defeats Satan.* Satan hates praise because Satan hates God and anything that exalts or pleases God. One of Satan's strategies is to get us to focus on ourselves—our needs, our problems, our circumstances, our feelings. When we lift our eyes up, though they may be filled with tears, and choose to praise the Lord, Satan's plan is defeated and God is victorious in our lives.

When Satan tempted Jesus to fall down and worship him, Jesus responded, "Thou shalt worship the Lord thy God" (Matthew 4:10 KJV). The moment that Jesus expressed His commitment to worship God alone, "the devil left him, and angels came and attended him" (4:11).

Has Satan tormented you with fears and doubts? Do you find yourself being bombarded with temptation to sin? Try praising the Lord, and watch Satan flee.

Finally, we should praise the Lord because *praise sets us free from spiritual bondage.* Ask Jonah. Sitting in the belly of that great fish, he began to cry out to the Lord, first in humility, then in worship. No sooner had the repenting prophet said, "With a song of thanksgiving, [I] will sacrifice to you" (Jonah 2:9), than "the LORD commanded the fish, and it vomited Jonah onto dry land" (2:10).

Praise precedes and prepares for deliverance. Ask Paul and Silas. In the middle of the night, prisoners in a Roman dungeon in Philippi, they turned their focus away from their wounds and looked heavenward with hymns of praise. God was so pleased that He sent a little heavenly accompaniment in the form of an earthquake that shook the foundations of the prison and caused the prison doors to fling wide open (Acts 16:11–34).

Are you living in some kind of prison? Perhaps you are in bondage to your past, to painful memories, to past failures, to the expectations of others, or to some sinful habit that enslaves you. Your prison may be the consequence of your own disobedience, as it was with Jonah. Or it may be the result of the wrongdoing of others, as in the case of Paul and Silas. If you have sinned, then, of course, repentance is the first step. Then lift up your heart from your prison cell, start to praise the Lord, and watch God begin to open the prison doors. Your circumstances may or may not change; but *you* will change—your heart will be released; God will set you free.

 Lifestyle of Praise

I want us to look, first, at some general, biblical principles regarding praise; then we will discover some practical ways we can express praise in our daily time alone with the Lord.

The Scripture teaches that praise, worship, and thanksgiving are to be the eternal occupation of every believer. Praise is not just an activity we do at scheduled times; it is to be *a continuous lifestyle.*

We have seen that the Old Testament priests offered up

"perpetual incense" to God every morning and every evening (Exodus 30:7–8 KJV), symbolizing the prayers and praise of God's people ascending to His throne. This incense was burned at the same time the oil lamps were lit, picturing that each time the lamp of God's Word is lit in our hearts, we are also to offer up prayers and praise to Him.

The importance of a continual lifestyle of praise is a recurring theme throughout both the Old and New Testaments:

> It is a good thing to give thanks unto the LORD, and to sing praise unto thy name, O most High: to shew forth thy lovingkindness in the morning, and thy faithfulness every night.

> I will bless the LORD at all times: his praise shall continually be in my mouth.

> Every day will I bless thee; and I will praise thy name for ever and ever.

> By [Jesus] therefore let us offer the sacrifice of praise to God continually, that is, the fruit of our lips giving thanks to his name.
> (PSALMS 92:1–2; 34:1; 145:2; HEBREWS 13:15; ALL KJV)

Praise is *an expression of faith and an act of the will*. It is not based on how we feel. David understood this concept as few others in the Scripture. In Psalm 34, we find David in one of the darkest periods of his life. Years earlier he had received God's promise that he was to be the next king, but the insecure egomaniac who occupied the throne was determined to take his life. So David found himself living as a fugitive in the wilderness, fleeing for his life. All the ingredients were there to set him up for a major depression. But instead, he made a choice—a choice to praise the Lord, regardless of his natural feelings:

> I will *bless the LORD at all times: his praise shall continually be in my mouth.* (PSALM 34:1 KJV, emphasis added)

When he decided to magnify the Lord instead of his circumstances, David's heart was lifted, as were the hearts of others around him:

> *My soul shall make her boast in the LORD: the humble ["the afflicted,"
> NIV] shall hear thereof, and be glad. O magnify the LORD with me, and
> let us exalt his name together.* (PSALM 34:2–3 KJV)

Praise is not a response to our circumstances, which constantly fluctuate. Praise is a response to the goodness and love of a God who never changes. That is why David could say,

> *My heart is fixed, O God, my heart is fixed: I will sing and give praise.*
> (PSALM 57:7 KJV)

It didn't matter to David whether he was sitting on the throne or being pursued by the one who was. It didn't matter whether he was hungry or full, happy or sad, alone or with friends. All that mattered was that God was there. And as long as God was there he could choose to praise.

Praise demonstrates faith that God is bigger and greater than any circumstance we may be facing. And faith pleases God—that is why He loves it when we choose to praise Him, regardless of how we feel.

Praise is *a ministry to God*. Praise is first and foremost for God, not for us. The purpose of praise is to bring *Him* blessing and pleasure, not to make *us* feel good. In our narcissistic, sensual culture, "praise and worship" has become for many believers a "spiritual," even erotic, expression of self-stimulation and self-love—a means of experiencing self-fulfillment. This is far from true worship and is not pleasing to the Lord.

In Exodus 30, God gave Moses the precise "recipe" for making the incense that was to be used in the temple worship. Then He emphasized:

> *It shall be most holy to you. Do not make any incense with this formu-*

la for yourselves; consider it holy to the LORD. Whoever makes any like it to enjoy its fragrance must be cut off from his people. (EXODUS 30:36–38)

Though true worship will bring about many benefits and blessings in our lives, the purpose of praise is not to satisfy us, but to bless Him.

Praise is to be *both public and private*, much as a husband and wife may display their affection for each other, both when they are in the company of others as well as when they are alone.

Many Scriptures speak of praising the Lord in the company of His people:

> Let them exalt him in the assembly of the people
> and praise him in the council of the elders. . . .

> With my mouth I will greatly extol the LORD;
> in the great throng I will praise him. . . .

> I will extol the LORD with all my heart
> in the council of the upright and in the assembly.

—PSALMS 107:32; 109:30; 111:1

At other times, praise is a private expression of love between our hearts and our Beloved. For example, though the biblical personage Daniel was a high-ranking government official, he carved time out of his busy schedule each day to offer up praise to the Lord: "Three times a day he got down on his knees and prayed, giving thanks to his God" (Daniel 6:10).

In much the same way, David said, "Seven times a day I praise you for your righteous laws" (Psalm 119:164).

Praise *requires personal participation*—it is not a spectator sport. Christian concerts, tapes, and CDs have mushroomed into a huge business. Unfortunately, they have also contributed to a spectator mind-set about praise and worship. Like the world around us, the Christian world has developed an addiction to being entertained. Just turn down the houselights, shine some spotlights on the stage, and let us sit back and watch the performance. At home or in the car, many believers are quick to turn on the radio or throw some CDs on the stereo so they can listen to others sing songs of praise; but they are far less apt to lift up their own voices to the Lord.

Look around the congregation during the worship service in the average church and notice how many people are just standing there with their hymnal or chorus book open, or watching the screen at the front, barely mouthing the words, much less singing aloud to the Lord. They are the product of a culture in which singing just isn't done much anymore and in which many people have never even learned *how* to sing.

But if there is one group of people in the world who ought to love to sing, it is those who have been redeemed, for they are the ones who truly have something to sing about. According to the apostle Paul, the singing of "psalms, hymns and spiritual songs" is a primary evidence of being filled with the Spirit and of having a grateful heart (Ephesians 5:19; Colossians 3:16).

The psalms of David represent one man's intensely personal response to what God had revealed to him about His heart and His ways. They are not a collection of someone else's songs that the psalmist merely listened to; they are songs he wrote and sang from his own heart to the Lord. Throughout the psalms, there is a sense of David's entering into worship with all his heart:

> Praise the LORD, O my soul;
> all my inmost being, praise his holy name. . . .
>
> I will praise you, O LORD, with all my heart;
> before the "gods" I will sing your praise.
> I will bow down toward your holy temple
> and will praise your name
> for your love and your faithfulness.
>
> —PSALMS 103:1; 138:1–2

Many years ago I had an experience I don't think I will ever forget. I was on the road, spending the night in the home of a friend. A black pastor and his wife, visiting from Nigeria, were also guests in the same home that night. In the middle of the night, I was awakened by a sound unlike anything I had heard before. In the bedroom next to mine, that dear couple was singing "How Great Thou Art"—slowly, loudly, with a heavy accent, and with all their hearts. I wasn't sure I hadn't died and gone to heaven!

That man and woman were not spectators. They were right there on the stage—active participants in the great eternal drama of praise, performing for a sacred audience of One.

> O that with yonder sacred throng
> We at His feet may fall!
> We'll join the everlasting song,
> And crown Him Lord of all!
>
> —EDWARD PERRONET (1726–92)

How to Praise?

So how do we worship the Lord in our daily time alone with Him? Remember that worship, praise, and thanksgiving are a response to God's revelation of Himself. As He shows Himself to you and speaks to you through His Word, you will find yourself wanting to respond to Him in praise—*verbal* or *visible* adoration of God for who He is and what He has done. Praise must be expressed outwardly. Approximately one hundred times in the Psalms we read the English phrase "Praise the LORD." The word translated "praise" is the Hebrew verb *ha-lal*, which means "to be clear; to shine; hence to make a show, to boast; and thus to be clamorously foolish; to rave; to celebrate."[1]

There are many different expressions of praise and worship taught and illustrated in the Scripture. Ask the Holy Spirit to direct you in your worship. Here are some of the ways He may lead you to respond.

USE DIFFERENT PHYSICAL POSITIONS

A variety of different physical postures can be used in worshiping the Lord. Kneeling or bowing before the Lord is a position I often find myself taking in my personal worship. This is a position that is frequently referred to in the Scripture:

> *Come, let us bow down in worship,*
> *let us kneel before the LORD our Maker.*
> —PSALM 95:6

> *When all the Israelites saw the fire coming down and the glory of the LORD above the temple, they knelt on the pavement with their faces to the ground, and they worshiped and gave thanks to the LORD, saying, "He is good; his love endures forever." (2 CHRONICLES 7:3)*

Twenty-nine times in the Psalms, when we read the phrase "bless the Lord," the Hebrew word *barak* is used in the original text, a word that means "to kneel; to bless God (as an act of adoration)."[2] Have you taken time to bless the Lord today? Regardless of what is going on in your life at this moment, God is good; He is worthy of your praise. Before reading any further, why not pause and take a few moments to kneel before the Lord? Bless Him, adore Him, worship Him.

Sometimes you may wish to stand before the Lord, as the Israelites did during the great revival in Nehemiah's day (Nehemiah 9:5) and at the dedication of the temple (2 Chronicles 7:6). Hymn writer James Montgomery (1771–1854) urges us to

> Stand up and bless the Lord,
> Ye people of His choice;
> Stand up and bless the Lord your God
> With heart and soul and voice.

Stand up and bless the Lord,
   The Lord your God adore;
Stand up and bless His glorious name
   Henceforth forevermore.

At other times, the vision of the holiness and greatness of God may move you to fall prostrate on your face before the Lord. The twenty-four elders who surround the throne in John's vision in Revelation "fall down before him who sits on the throne, and worship him who lives for ever and ever" (Revelation 4:10).

The Scripture speaks of another physical expression of worship that involves the use of our hands. Psalm 47:1 tells us to "clap" our hands in praise to the Lord. The idea behind clapping our hands is not just to keep time or add rhythm to our singing. Nor is the purpose of clapping to generate an enthusiastic atmosphere.

When I think of clapping to the Lord, I think of a small child who claps with glee as she steps into the waves lapping the beach or as she opens a brightly wrapped box under the Christmas tree and is delighted to discover the doll she has been longing to own. I think of the applause of an adoring throng when the king comes out on the balcony and warmly greets his subjects.

Clapping to the Lord is the spontaneous, gleeful response of the sons and daughters of God when they step into the river of His delights or they have just discovered a gift of His grace. It is the passionate, heartfelt response of the subjects of King Jesus when He steps into their midst and touches their lives with His presence and His love.

Not only can we use our hands to clap to the Lord, but Psalm 134:2 speaks of lifting our hands to the Lord. Now, depending on your background, this one may be a little hard to swallow. For some in the body of Christ, this expression of worship has become a practice to which little thought or meaning is attached. On the other hand, some have rejected it

as extreme or sensational, while others have ignored it altogether. However, the practice of lifting of hands to the Lord
does not belong to one particular theological camp. Fifty
times in the Psalms the word *praise* is used to translate a Hebrew word that means "to revere or worship with extended
hands."[3]

The lifting of hands to the Lord is a deeply meaningful expression of worship that is meant to signify that God is high
and lifted up, that we are infinitely beneath Him, that we are
dependent upon Him, and that we acknowledge His right to
rule over us. Hands lifted up to the Lord say, "I surrender all,
Your Majesty."

Of course, no physical position is inherently more worshipful than another. The outward posture is merely intended
to express—or help cultivate within us—a heart attitude of
surrender and reverence.

SPEAK TO THE LORD

We can use our mouths to express love, praise, and thanksgiving to the Lord.

> *I will speak of the glorious honour of thy majesty, and of thy wondrous
> works. . . . My mouth shall speak the praise of the LORD.* (PSALM 145:5,
> 21 KJV)

Frequently, as I am reading a passage of Scripture that reveals to me something of the heart and ways of God or the
beauty of the Lord Jesus, I pause to respond by blessing the
Lord for what I have just read.

For example, this week I have been memorizing and meditating on the Song of Solomon. When I come to the last paragraph of chapter 5, where the bride describes what it is that
she admires about her Beloved, I find myself using some of
those very words to express my admiration of the Lord Jesus:

"O, my Beloved, You are radiant and dazzling; You shine so brightly because You are the radiance of the Father's glory. You truly are the 'chiefest among ten thousand'; there is none like You; no one can be compared with You. Everything about You is perfect and lovely and beautiful. There is no flaw in You. Your countenance is excellent. Your mouth is most sweet; yes, You are altogether lovely, my Beloved and my Friend."

Another passage I meditated on this morning evoked praise from my heart:

I will bear the indignation of the LORD, because I have sinned against him, until he plead my cause, and execute judgment for me: he will bring me forth to the light, and I shall behold his righteousness. (MICAH 7:9 KJV)

As I read that verse, I was reminded of the terrible consequences of sin—*my* sin—and that I would have to bear those consequences myself, were it not for One who was willing to plead my cause and take my judgment upon Himself. I began to praise God for the cross of Christ where the blameless Son of God became sin for me and bore on Himself the full wrath of God against my sin. As a result of His sacrificial death on my behalf, I do not have to fear death, for I have received eternal life. "Thank You, Lord, that You will bring me forth to the light—Your eternal dwelling place—and that, by Your grace, I will behold Your righteousness forever."

Sometimes I bless the Lord with my mouth by reading aloud portions of the Psalms or other passages that are directed to Him. At other times, I simply voice my own words of praise to Him. As the hymn exhorts us:

Tell out, my soul, the greatness of the Lord!
    Unnumbered blessings give my spirit voice;
Tender to me the promise of His Word;
    In God my Savior shall my heart rejoice.

—TIMOTHY DUDLEY-SMITH (1926–)[4]

A variation on speaking to the Lord is *shouting to the Lord.* Now it's not that God is hard of hearing. But sometimes our joy in Him may only be able to be expressed in loud exclamations. Psalm 32:11 (KJV) tells us to "shout for joy, all ye that are upright in heart." The Hebrew word that is translated "shout" in that verse is a word that means "to creak; to shout for joy."[5] (Numerous times in the Psalms, the same Hebrew word is translated "sing," as in Psalm 30:4.) A different word is used in Psalm 47:1 (KJV; "shout unto God with the voice of triumph"). This word means "to split the ears with sound."[6]

SING TO THE LORD

This is one of my favorite expressions of praise, and one that I believe merits special attention beyond what has already been said in this chapter. In the Psalms alone, there are sixty-eight references to singing to the Lord. We are told to sing praises to the Lord, to sing aloud of His righteousness, to sing of His power, to sing aloud of His mercy, to sing forth the honor of His name, to sing for joy, to sing of mercy and judgment, to sing a new song unto the Lord, to sing psalms unto Him, to sing the Lord's song in a strange land, and to sing aloud upon our beds.

I travel a great deal, but I hardly ever go anywhere without taking along a hymnal and a book of worship choruses. More days than not, I will take time to sing several hymns or songs to the Lord. Over the years, I have sung through literally thousands of hymns and songs, using a variety of old and newer hymnals. I make a practice of singing all the stanzas and then jotting down the date on which I sang that particular hymn or song. Next to reading the Bible itself, singing—both to and about the Lord—has probably been the activity that has produced the greatest encouragement, blessing, and joy in my Christian walk.

Many of the repetitive, simple choruses that we sing today are meaningful expressions of love and devotion to the Lord. But if we limit our diet to those choruses, I believe we are missing out on a precious treasure God has given to the church.

Many of the hymns and spiritual songs written throughout the history of the church are rich in theology; they communicate God's nature and redemptive plan with a depth that is not commonly found in the most popular choruses and songs of our day. Disposing of those hymns can easily lead to a spiritual experience that is shallow, trite, self-centered, and emotionally driven. It may take more thought and effort to sing "A Mighty Fortress Is Our God" or "Jesus, the Very Thought of Thee" than to sing some of our contemporary choruses, but the long-term payoff of disciplining our minds to think (and sing) great thoughts about God is well worth the effort.

Singing to the Lord is a powerful weapon in overcoming the Enemy. Apparently, before he exalted himself against God and was cast out of heaven, Lucifer had a major role in leading the music and worship of heaven ("the workmanship of thy tabrets and of thy pipes was prepared in thee in the day that thou wast created" ([Ezekiel 28:13 KJV]). Now, as a fallen creature, he knows the power of music as a means of praise. He knows how much God loves to hear the musical praises of His creatures. He knows the power of praise to deliver us from bondage. So he strives to keep us from singing or to cause us to make music for our own pleasure and gratification rather than to magnify and exalt the Lord.

Over and over again, I have seen the power of singing to defeat Satan and to overcome emotional bondage that he may have led us into. Discouragement, fear, anxiety, depression, grief—in many cases, these will flee as we sing to the Lord. On occasion, I have felt as if an enormous dark cloud were hanging over my spirit. Invariably, as I have sung to the Lord—sometimes with a trembling voice—the cloud has lifted and the sunlight of His sweet peace and grace has poured in, quickening and encouraging my heart.

Some time ago, I had the privilege of participating in the weekly Tuesday evening prayer meeting at the Brooklyn Tabernacle in New York City. I arrived several minutes after the service had already begun, to find the auditorium packed with wall-to-wall people. The audience was extremely diverse— "red and yellow, black and white," old and young, professionals and blue-collar workers, well dressed and poorly dressed— side by side, they praised and prayed together.

One of the things that particularly touched me was the singing. The singing was so earnest and full that at times it sounded like peals of thunder or as if a freight train had driven through the room. It has been a long time since I have heard such uninhibited, heartfelt singing. I was reminded of that occasion during the great revival in Nehemiah's day, when "the singers sang loud, . . . so that the joy of Jerusalem was heard even afar off" (Nehemiah 12:42–43 KJV).

When I learned something of the people who were in the audience that night, I understood better why they sang as they did. Many of the men and women in that church have come to Christ out of backgrounds of drug addiction, alcoholism, violent crime, and sexual promiscuity. They know what it is to be enslaved to sin. They know what it is to be without hope and without Christ.

And they know what it is to have God reach down and rescue them by His grace. They know what it is to be "redeemed by the blood of the Lamb." They have not forgotten where God found them. When they sing about the love and the mercy and the greatness of God, they know what they are singing about. And they sing like they mean it. Because they do.

> Praise, my soul, the King of heaven,
>   To His feet thy tribute bring;
> Ransomed, healed, restored, forgiven,
>   Evermore His praises sing;
> Alleluia! Alleluia!
>   Praise the everlasting King.
>
> —HENRY F. LYTE (1793–1847)

MAKING IT PERSONAL

1. Of the various expressions of praise referred to in this chapter, which ones are you most accustomed to? Which ones are you least comfortable with? Why?

2. What are some of the obstacles you have experienced that have made it difficult to praise the Lord with all your heart?

    What have you learned in this chapter that has motivated you to cultivate a lifestyle of praise and worship?

3. Read Psalm 145 aloud.

    • What does this passage reveal about what God is like and what He has done? Make a list.
    • Pray this psalm back to God, personalizing it and praising Him for each of His attributes and blessings (for example, verse 8: "Lord, I praise You for the grace and compassion that You have poured out on me—You have given me so much more than I deserve; Your love toward me is greater than any other love I have ever known . . .").

4. Write your own psalm of praise, thanking God for His character, for His works on your behalf, and for physical and spiritual blessings you have received from Him.

5. Sing at least one psalm or hymn to the Lord each day for the next week. You may want to sing out of a hymnal, make up a tune for one of your favorite psalms, or even compose your own lyrics and sing them to the Lord.

Kay Arthur

Worship lifts our focus off of man and the circumstances of life and puts it on God, who rules over every circumstance. It causes us to turn our attention to heaven and the eternal, giving us sweet relief from earth and the temporal.

Oh, beloved, worship is an essential element in your quiet time alone with God if you want to experience the abundance of life and peace that is the birthright of every child of God, for it puts everything into proper perspective as you acknowledge Him.

Worship means to bow down; therefore, to me the essence of true worship is to recognize God as God, to admire Him in all His beauty, and to submit myself totally to Him. Thus, in worship you might try taking this posture: on your knees or even flat on your face before Him. There have been times when I slipped to my knees because I have literally felt uncomfortable sitting. Then there have been times when I have felt the need to stretch out on my face before Him.

And what brings me to this position? Primarily, the Word of God, for it is here that I see God as He really is. To acknowledge His Word as true and to submit to what that means—to me this is the highest form of worship.

In addition to the Bible, a hymnal is a wonderful help in worship for many people, for the hymns of old are rich in biblical truth. You can simply read the hymns, joining the hymn writer in rehearsing the goodness of God and His wondrous ways in the affairs of men.

Or you can use the hymnbook of the Bible, the book of Psalms. If you use one psalm a day for worship, in five months you will have read through the book of Psalms.

Another way to worship the Lord is through music. The richer the doctrine, the more my spirit soars, for I am singing truth. There have been times in my life when my heart was so full of rejoicing that I literally made up songs as I simply began singing the words that were on my heart. I have to admit that they were never songs that one would publish! However, I am sure that both words and melody were precious in the ears of my Father because they flowed from the grateful heart of one of His children.

Worship is my means of coming into His presence and acknowledging why I am there! I am there at His feet because He is God and there is no other . . . the Sovereign Ruler of the universe, my Creator, my Sustainer, my Life, my Salvation, Abba Father . . . whose mercies are new every morning. From worship, my heart is prepared to move on to submission and petition.[7]

☐ ☐ ☐ ──

Kay Arthur and her husband, Jack, are cofounders of Precept Ministries. God has used Kay's writing and teaching ministry to challenge thousands of believers to study His Word for themselves and to apply it to their lives.

NOTES

PART PAGE: George Müller, in *Spiritual Secrets of George Müller*, ed. Roger Steer (Wheaton: Harold Shaw, 1985), 61.

1. *Strong's Exhaustive Concordance* (Grand Rapids: Baker, 1982).
2. Ibid.
3. Ibid.
4. "Tell Out, My Soul," by Timothy Dudley-Smith. © 1962 Hope Publishing Co., Carol Stream, IL 60188. All rights reserved. Used by permission.
5. *Strong's Exhaustive Concordance.*
6. Ibid.
7. Adapted from *A Quiet Time Alone with God* by Kay Arthur, published by Precept Ministries, 1986. Used by permission.

CHAPTER 11

The Privilege of Prayer: A Longing Cry

"My most important appointment today is with Jesus in prayer."

Every morning as I settle into my quiet-time chair to meet with the Lord, I see those words on a plaque given to me by a praying friend. I need that crucial reminder, as my mind so easily drifts off to other "important appointments" and tasks that lie ahead.

The truth is, all too often I find myself in a hurry to "get through" my devotions, so I can move on to the other demands and business of the day. But when I look at that plaque, I am forced to stop and take stock and to face God's perspective of what really matters. As Jesus said to that first-century homemaker who was harried and uptight about getting her "to do" list all checked off,

> *"Martha, Martha, . . . you are worried and upset about many things, but only one thing is needed. Mary has chosen what is better, and it will not be taken away from her."* (LUKE 10:41–42, emphasis added)

Without question, this chapter has been the most difficult one of this book for me to write. Perhaps I should begin by just admitting that throughout my entire spiritual pilgrimage, prayer has been a struggle for me. I have always loved to read, study, memorize, and meditate on the Word. But prayer has never come easily for me.

Loving biographies as I do, I am well aware that great men and women of God have been men and women of prayer. I have been inspired by the accounts of their prayer life, but have also felt like an infant when I considered my prayer life next to theirs.

As I write, I am pulled by two conflicting desires. On the one hand, I do not want to leave a better impression of my own prayer life than is honestly true, nor do I want to attempt to instruct others beyond where I have walked myself. At the same time, I want to convince you of what I know in my heart to be true—that rich communion with God in prayer can be a daily reality and practice in each of our lives.

Prayerlessness

Several years ago, the Lord began to speak to me about my prayerlessness. It's not that I *never* prayed—I tried to live each day in a spirit of prayer, seeking to know the heart and mind of God in relation to my activities and relationships and to know what would please Him in each decision and circumstance. But, with few exceptions over the years, I had never cultivated a practice of set times for private prayer. Others may have assumed that I was a woman of prayer; but God knew and I knew that was not the case.

I'd like to say that what followed was a major breakthrough that resulted in my becoming the prayer warrior I wanted to be. In my case, there has been no such breakthrough. However, what God began in my heart that summer has been an ongoing process that has included both a measure of growth as well as seasons of defeat. As Charles Swindoll would say, it has been "three steps forward and two steps back." I do know that there is deep within my heart a call and a commitment to press on, to lay hold of the heart and hand of God through prayer.

As God opened my eyes to this matter of prayerlessness, I asked Him to let me see it from His point of view. Here is what I wrote in my journal one day when God first began to deal with my heart:

I am convicted that prayerlessness . . .

— is a sin against God (1 Samuel 12:23).
— is direct disobedience to the command of Christ ("watch and pray," Matthew 26:41).
— is direct disobedience to the Word of God ("pray without ceasing," 1 Thessalonians 5:17 KJV).
— makes me vulnerable to temptation ("watch and pray so that you will not fall into temptation," Matthew 26:41).
— expresses independence—no need for God.
— gives place to the Enemy and makes me vulnerable to his schemes (Ephesians 6:10–20; Daniel 10).
— results in powerlessness.
— limits (and defines) my relationship with God.
— hinders me from knowing His will, His priorities, His direction.
— forces me to operate in the realm of the natural (what I can do) versus the supernatural (what He can do).
— leaves me weak, harried, and hassled.
— is rooted in pride, self-sufficiency, laziness, and lack of discipline.
— reveals a lack of real burden and compassion for others.

Why We Don't Pray

Since that time, I have pondered the question: Why don't we pray more? Why don't I pray more? Here is what I have come to believe is the number one reason for my own prayerlessness:

We don't pray because we are not desperate. We're not really conscious of our *need* for God. Puritan pastor William Gurnall makes this point in his writings:

> Perhaps the deadness of thy heart in prayer ariseth from not having a deep sense of thy wants, and the mercies thou art in need of. . . . The hungry man needs no help to teach him how to beg.[1]

In the last chapter I mentioned visiting the Brooklyn Tabernacle, a church that is known as a praying church. Pastor Jim Cymbala explained to us why it's not hard for his people to pray: "In our prayer meetings, you've got *desperate people* crying out to God. Some of them don't have jobs. Others have husbands who are alcoholics or strung out on drugs. Many are women with no husband at all, trying to raise their children on welfare. Every day we are dealing with crack/cocaine addicts, AIDS patients, people who are HIV positive, people who have never had any family to speak of—these people are desperate! They *need* God; they don't have anywhere else to turn. That's why they pray."

In comparison to many of the people who attend the Brooklyn Tabernacle, my life has been relatively trouble-free. I have never had to wonder where the next meal is coming from—so why would I be desperate to pray, "Give us this day our daily bread"? From a human standpoint, I can live my life without God's help. I can operate, humanly speaking, on my own efforts, my own resources, apart from His grace and intervention.

I have a dear friend whose third child was born with multiple birth defects, including the fact that he had no esophagus. For years, her son was in critical condition, in and out of hospitals, undergoing life-threatening surgeries, requiring a breathing apparatus every night, prone to choking, and frequently unable to breathe. Do you think anyone had to tell that mother to pray for her son? On the contrary, you couldn't keep her from praying—she was desperate; she knew her son's only hope of survival was for God to intervene and spare his life; she knew the only way she could get through those years of sleepless nights was for God to pour His grace into her life and grant supernatural strength and enabling.

Though my natural instinct is to wish for a life free from pain, trouble, and adversity, I am learning to welcome anything that makes me conscious of my need for Him. If prayer is birthed out of desperation, then anything that makes me desperate for God is a blessing.

How Can I Pray?

As I have moved toward God in prayer, I have been helped by the following suggestions.

ASK THE LORD JESUS TO TEACH YOU TO PRAY

When the disciples saw Jesus' prayer life, they were moved to plead with Him, "Lord, teach *us* to pray." And He did. Along with those disciples, I have studied the prayer life of the Lord Jesus. I have been touched by the intimate communion He shared with His heavenly Father. And I have cried out to Him, "Lord, please teach *me* to pray."

ASK THE HOLY SPIRIT TO HELP YOU PRAY

It is encouraging to me to know that someone as great as the apostle Paul would confess, "We do not know what we ought to pray for" (Romans 8:26). He recognized his need for help in knowing how to pray according to the will of God. But he also recognized that God had made a provision for his need, that the Holy Spirit had been given as a Helper:

> *The Spirit helps us in our weakness. We do not know what we ought to pray for, but the Spirit himself intercedes for us with groans that words cannot express. And he who searches our hearts knows the mind of the Spirit, because the Spirit intercedes for the saints in accordance with God's will.* (ROMANS 8:26–27)

At times, as you are praying for a particular individual or concern, you may need to say, "Holy Spirit, I do not know the will of the Father on this matter. I do not know how to pray. But the Word says that You will help me in my weakness, that You will intercede for me in accordance with the will of God. I ask You to do that now; I need You; please express to the Father what You know to be His will."

PRAY THE WORD OF GOD BACK TO GOD

We all know that we are to pray "according to the will of God." But how can we know His will? There are many matters on which it may be difficult to know the will of God. But we can be sure of one thing, and that is that the Word of God is the will of God. When we pray the Word of God back to God, we can be sure we are praying according to His will. Two scriptural examples come to mind.

Second Samuel 7 records the occasion when David was seeking to know God's will regarding his desire to build a temple for God. In this case, God revealed His will to David through the prophet Nathan. The word came back from God to David that he was not the one God had chosen to build a house for Him, but that David's son would be the one to build the house. Then God promised David that He would establish and bless him and his family and that David's family line would always have a king to sit on the throne: "Your house and your kingdom will endure forever before me; your throne will be established forever" (2 Samuel 7:16).

Verses 18–29 record the prayer that David prayed in response to the words God had spoken to him. He begins by expressing wonder and gratitude that God would deal so graciously with His servant. He worships God: "How great you are, O Sovereign Lord! There is no one like you, and there is no God but you" (2 Samuel 7:22).

Then he goes on to make his petition to the Lord. His whole petition is based on what God has already promised him. He merely asks God to keep His own Word.

THE PRIVILEGE OF PRAYER 237

"And now, LORD God, keep forever the promise you have made concerning your servant and his house. Do as you promised, so that your name will be great forever. Then men will say, 'The Lord Almighty is God over Israel!' . . .

"O LORD Almighty, God of Israel, you have revealed this to your servant, saying, 'I will build a house for you.' So your servant has found courage to offer you this prayer. O Sovereign LORD, You are God! Your words are trustworthy, and you have promised these good things to your servant. Now be pleased to bless the house of your servant, that it may continue forever in your sight: for you, O Sovereign LORD, have spoken." (2 SAMUEL 7:25–29)

What is David saying? "Lord, I'm asking You to do what You have already promised to do. I dare to ask boldly because You have told me this is Your will."

Daniel was another man who knew how to pray according to God's Word. Daniel 9:2–3 illustrates how Daniel prayed this way (emphasis added):

I, Daniel, understood from the Scriptures, according to the word of the LORD given to Jeremiah the prophet, that the desolation of Jerusalem would last seventy years. So I turned to the Lord God and pleaded with him in prayer and petition, in fasting, and in sackcloth and ashes.

How did Daniel know what to pray? He prayed according to the Word of God that had already been revealed. When he read Jeremiah's prophecy that said the Jewish nation would be in exile for seventy years, he began to pray that God would deliver His people from captivity.

Knowing the outcome (that the captivity would last for seventy years) did not cause Daniel to sit back and wait for it to happen. Rather, knowing the will of God motivated him to pray more fervently:

"For Your sake, O Lord, look with favor on your desolate sanctuary. Give

ear, O God, and hear; open your eyes and see the desolation of the city that bears your Name. . . . O Lord, listen! O Lord, forgive! O Lord, hear and act! For your sake, O my God, do not delay." (DANIEL 9:17–19)

Daniel prayed according to the Scriptures he had read. He prayed for God's will—as it had already been revealed—to be done on earth. In his prayer, Daniel aligned himself with the heart, the plan, and the purposes of God. Through prayer, he became a partner with God in the fulfilling of those purposes.

There is nothing wrong with letting the Lord know the desires and requests that are on our hearts. In fact, He tells us to "pray about everything" (Philippians 4:6 TLB).

But when we lay hold of His will as He has expressed it in His Word, we can pray boldly, with confidence that He not only hears, but that He will grant those things we have asked of Him (1 John 5:14–15).

For example, I have some dear friends whose marriage is in major trouble. I often feel at a loss as to exactly how to pray for them. But I know I can pray confidently when I pray according to God's will as it is revealed in His Word. I know it is God's will for this husband to love his wife in the same selfless, sacrificing, serving way that Jesus loves His church (Ephesians 5:25). I know it is God's will for him to dwell with his wife in an understanding way and to honor her (1 Peter 3:7). I know it is God's will for this wife to reverence her husband, regardless of his faults and failures, and to submit to his leadership in the home (Ephesians 5:22–33). I know it is God's will that they would walk in love, in oneness, and in truth. I pray these and other passages for this couple, calling upon God to fulfill in them His revealed will.

When I am considering a purchase, I feel great freedom to make my request known to the Lord. But I do not necessarily feel the freedom to claim that the request will be granted. What I can pray with confidence is that the Lord will direct my steps (as He has promised to do), that He will cleanse my heart from any wrong motives, that He will protect me from selfish desires or from anything that might be harmful to my walk with Him, that He will grant me wisdom as I make the decision, that He will be glorified in the outcome, and that I will have a contented and grateful heart, whether or not He chooses to provide the item I have desired. These are all requests I know to be according to the will of God, and I can boldly ask Him to fulfill His will.

What Should We Pray For?

Many people find it helpful to use some sort of prayer list to organize their prayer life. Others feel that such lists tend to make their praying more mechanical and perfunctory, preferring instead to let God use His Word and His Spirit to prompt them about the things they ought to pray for that day.

Regardless of whether or not you choose to use a prayer list, there are several categories of prayer requests that we ought to pray for on a regular basis.

PRAY FOR THE ADVANCEMENT
OF CHRIST'S KINGDOM IN THE WORLD

The first three petitions of the Lord's Prayer focus on this concern.

> *"Hallowed be Thy Name."* Your Name is holy. May Your Name be worshiped and honored by Your people everywhere. May our lives in no way bring disrespect or dishonor to Your great Name. And may all peoples of the earth come to revere Your sacred Name.
>
> *"Thy kingdom come."* "Your kingdom is an everlasting kingdom, and Your dominion endures through all generations. . . . [You] will rule from sea to sea" (Psalms 145:13; 72:8). May Your kingdom be established throughout this entire world. May You rule and reign supreme this day in my heart and in the hearts of Your people. And haste the day when "the kingdoms of this world [will] become the kingdoms of our Lord, and . . . [You will] reign for ever and ever" (Revelation 11:15 KJV).

"Thy will be done on earth as it is in heaven." May You have Your way this day in my life and in the lives of Your people throughout the earth. May we live in submission to You, even as the hosts of heaven seek only to know and to do Your good pleasure (Psalm 103:21). Fulfill all Your holy purposes in the nations and peoples of the earth this day.

In offering up these petitions to God, we are making His priorities our priorities. We are saying that what matters most to Him matters most to us. We are subordinating our own personal needs and agenda to the wider concerns of His kingdom.

In his classic book *Quiet Talks on Prayer,* S. D. Gordon captures the significance and profound effect of this kind of "kingdom praying":

> Prayer . . . is an insistent claiming, by a man . . . down on the contested earth, that the power of Jesus' victory over the great evil-spirit chieftain shall extend to particular lives now under his control. . . .
>
> Prayer is insisting upon Jesus' victory, and the retreat of the enemy on each particular spot and heart and problem concerned. . . . Prayer is man giving God a footing on the contested territory of this earth. . . .
>
> Prayer opens a whole planet to a man's activities. I can as really be touching hearts for God in far away India or China through prayer, as though I were there.[2]

PRAY FOR OTHERS

In my case, those "others" include family members, friends, the staff of the ministry in which I serve, pastors and Christian leaders, our president and other elected officials, and non-Christian neighbors and friends.

As you pray for people that God lays on your heart, you may feel prompted to stop and jot a note to one or more individuals that you sense need special encouragement. The note may express appreciation for their life or ministry, or it may just let them know that you have prayed for them that day. (I keep a basket of note cards next to my quiet-time chair for this purpose.)

On Sunday mornings, I generally take time to intercede for my pastor, for the pastors of other local churches in my community, and for numerous other pastors throughout the country that God has laid on my heart. I pray that they will be anointed servants of the Lord, that their hearts and motives will be pure, that they will not fear man but will fear only the Lord, that they will boldly proclaim the truth of His Word, that God will encourage them in their ministry, and that those who listen to them preach will tremble at the Word of the Lord and will have ears to hear and hearts to respond to what God says through His servants.

God has been gracious to raise up around me an incredible team of praying men and women. Many of those individuals, some of whom do not even know me well, have shared that they pray for me *every single day*. I cannot imagine what blessing and protection I would be missing if it were not for their faithful, fervent prayers on my behalf. The impact of their prayers on my life motivates me to intercede on behalf of those that God has put on my heart.

I do not think we can really begin to fathom the effect that may be had on the lives of others through our prayers. As Andrew Bonar points out: "How much we may be to blame for the faults of others not being cured! We point to their faults and failings, but we don't pray for them."[3]

Let me say a special word of encouragement to mothers or grandmothers who are carrying a burden for your children or grandchildren—especially those who may be far from the Lord. You may be crying yourself to sleep at night over their condition; you may be at your wit's end; you may have nowhere to turn for help. But whatever you do, don't stop praying.

In a sense, I believe my life is the product of a praying great-grandmother. I never met *Yaya*, my father's Greek immigrant grandmother. But I know that she was a praying woman. After coming to America, Yaya and her husband lived in a house in upstate New York with their two sons, two daughters-in-law (who were sisters), and four grandsons. One of those grandchildren, my dad's cousin, Ted DeMoss, shared a bedroom with Yaya when he was a little boy. Before he went to heaven, I recall hearing Ted tell of nights when Yaya would be on her knees praying in her native tongue as he went to sleep. She was praying for the salvation of her children and grandchildren. On some mornings, Ted told us, he would awaken and Yaya would still be on her knees, praying for her family.

Eventually, all four of those boys came to faith in Christ. I believe my father's dramatic conversion in 1950 was an answer to Yaya's prayers. Likewise, I believe that the literally dozens of Yaya's great-grandchildren and great-great-grandchildren who are walking with the Lord today are the fruit of her faithful prayers.

You may have no idea when or how God will answer your prayers, but *don't stop praying.* Andrew Bonar gives this word of encouragement when the answer to our prayers is delayed: "The blessing we pray for may not come at once, but it is on its way. Sometimes the Lord keeps us waiting long, because He likes to keep us in His presence."[4]

PRAY FOR YOURSELF

"But isn't that selfish?" you may wonder. Not if your motive is that God be glorified through your life. On a day-to-day basis, there are many personal matters that I lay before the Lord. I seek His direction in relation to my schedule, my priorities, my relationships, my work, and my physical and spiritual needs. As I pray, I try to listen to the Lord and to be sensitive to how He may be directing my mind in relation to that matter. For example, on a recent morning, as I was praying for direction on a specific issue, I felt impressed to call a particular individual to ask for prayer and input. I believe the Lord brought that person's name to mind as I was praying, and that He will use that friend's prayerful counsel to help direct my steps.

There are several personal petitions I make to the Lord

more often than any others. Through the years, these are things that I have prayed over and over again.

Guard my heart. Make and keep it pure. Guard my motives, my attitudes, my values, and my responses to the circumstances of life. Protect me from the schemes and attacks of the Evil One.

Fill me with Your love. Help me to love You with all my heart, soul, mind, and strength. Make me compassionate and sensitive to the needs of others around me. Help me to give of myself to meet the needs of others, without expecting anything in return.

Fill me with Your Spirit. May I be emptied of myself and filled with Jesus. May my life be lived in the realm of the supernatural. Anoint my life and ministry with supernatural power.

Clothe me in humility. May I be broken—poor in spirit—toward You and toward all others. May I esteem all others as better than myself. May I not seek to impress others, but only to please You.

Make me a servant. Help me to serve You with gladness; to render each act of service as unto Christ; to joyously accept even "menial" or "unfulfilling" responsibilities. Help me to serve heartily, happily, humbly.

Guard my tongue. "Set a watch, O LORD, before my mouth; keep the door of my lips" (Psalm 141:3 KJV). May I speak only words that are true, words that help and heal, words that are wise and kind (Proverbs 31:26).

Give me wisdom and discernment. Help me to see all of life from Your point of view. May my life be ruled by the wisdom of Your Word. Give me the "wisdom that is from above . . . pure, then peaceable, gentle, and easy to be intreated, full of mercy and good fruits, without partiality, and without hypocrisy" (James 3:17 KJV).

Give me a grateful spirit, a thankful heart. Help me to give thanks in everything. Help me to acknowledge and express the benefits and blessings that I have received from You and others. Protect me from a discontented heart and a murmuring tongue.

Help me to walk by faith and not by sight. May my life show the world how great, how good, and how powerful You are. May I be willing to step out in faith when I cannot see the outcome, and may my life not be explainable in human terms.

Teach me the fear of the Lord. Help me to practice the conscious, constant awareness that You see, hear, and know all. Help me to live my life in light of the final judgment and as one who will give account to You.

"WHAT IS THY PETITION? . . . IT SHALL BE GRANTED THEE."

The book of Esther is one of my favorites for many reasons. But one of the most meaningful personal applications I have found in that book is the insight it provides on prayer.

Totally apart from any initiative or effort on her part, God sovereignly arranged for Esther to be placed in a position of great influence at a crucial moment in Israel's history. Esther couldn't see the script God had written in heaven and was carrying out on earth. The entire Jewish nation stood in the balance, as wicked Haman set out to destroy the chosen people of God. For a brief time, from earth's vantage point, it seemed he was going to succeed. (When you look around and it appears that the Enemy has God in a checkmate position, do not despair. Remember, we see things from a limited, finite point of view. God is still on His throne, and His purposes will not be thwarted.)

You know the story. When Mordecai, Esther's cousin and the object of Haman's hatred, discovered the insidious plot to annihilate the Jews, he immediately appealed to Queen Esther to exercise her royal position by interceding before King Artaxerxes on behalf of her people.

Esther's initial hesitation stemmed from one important fact. She knew that no one dared approach the king without being invited. To do so was to risk death—unless the king was to have mercy and extend his golden scepter in welcome. She knew her life would be in jeopardy if she were to initiate an audience with the king.

Mordecai finally persuaded Esther that she had been placed in this position for a purpose greater than herself and that she simply must get involved. After three days of fasting, Esther put on her royal robes and went into the inner court of the palace where the king sat on his throne. I love those next two verses:

> *And it was so, when the king saw Esther the queen standing in the court, that* she *obtained favour in his sight: and the king held out to*

Esther the golden sceptre that was in his hand. So Esther drew near, and touched the top of the sceptre. Then said the king unto her, What wilt thou, queen Esther? and what is thy request? it shall be even given thee to the half of the kingdom. (ESTHER 5:2–3 KJV, emphasis added)

Here we have a glimpse into the incredible relationship between an all-powerful God, who sits on His throne in heaven, and believers who approach His throne from their position on earth to intercede on behalf of His people. (The analogy is not complete because, of course, Artaxerxes, being a pagan king, cannot possibly represent God accurately.)

When we, like Queen Esther, become aware of a need here on earth, we may be reluctant to approach the King of the universe with our puny needs and burdens. But we forget that this King loves us, He has chosen us, He delights in us, and, inexplicably, He has determined to accomplish His purposes on earth in union with the prayers of His people. In fact, He is *waiting* for us to come and ask.

We may be fearful to approach One who is so powerful and who could destroy us with a flicker of His eyelids, should He so choose. But when we approach His throne, "clothed in His righteousness alone" (even as Esther prepared by putting on her royal robes), wonder of wonders, we obtain "favor in His sight," He extends His golden scepter toward us, and we are welcomed to draw near and touch the top of the scepter.

Having granted us access into His presence, the King then says to us, "What is your request, my beloved? It shall be given you. Ask, and you will receive."

As the story of Esther progresses, King Artaxerxes asks her the same question three more times (Esther 5:6; 7:2; 9:12), assuring her that there is no limit to his generosity, his desire to bless her, and his ability to fulfill any request she may make — whatever she asks will be granted.

I often wonder what supernatural acts God would perform in our world — things He is ready, willing, eager, and able to do — if we would just approach Him and make our requests

A PLACE OF QUIET REST

known. What wonders and blessings does He wish to release that await only the heart-cry of one of His subjects down here on earth?

Years ago, a friend raised this question, which has stayed in my mind: If God only did that in my life and the lives of others which I asked Him to do, how much would He do? And how much more might we receive from His hand, if only we prayed more?

> Thou art coming to a King;
>   Large petitions with thee bring.
> For His grace and pow'r are such
>   None can ever ask too much!

—JOHN NEWTON (1725–1807)

O God, make us desperate, and grant us faith and boldness to approach Your throne and make our petitions known, knowing that in so doing we link arms with Omnipotence and become instruments of Your eternal purposes being fulfilled on this earth.

MAKING IT PERSONAL

1. What are the biggest battles you face in your prayer life? What keeps you from approaching His throne to make your petitions?

2. What are you asking God for that only He can do?

3. Read Paul's prayer in Ephesians 3:14–21. Now make this your prayer. Pray these words on behalf of a family member, a friend, or your pastor.

4. If Jesus were to say to you, as He did to the blind beggar in Luke 18:41, "What do you want me to do for you?" how would you answer Him? What would you like to believe God to do in your life? in your family? in your church? in your community and nation?

FROM THE HEART OF

Jeanne Seaborn

I have a prayer notebook that has evolved over the years. In addition to praying for different ministries and people each day, I organize my prayers for my children and grandchildren. At the beginning of each year, I ask each child and grandchild to write down their main prayer requests for the year. I pray these for them each day.

In addition, I have a page for each child and grandchild with Scriptures that I pray especially for them. Each day I pray in-depth for one child, using those verses. For example, for my son-in-law who travels during the week, I pray Psalm 119:54: "Your decrees are the theme of my song wherever I lodge." Each child has at least one verse dealing with keeping a clear conscience, as well as other verses that I personalize and pray back to God for that individual. I believe in praying Scripture for family members, because God honors His Word.

Each year I set a character goal, a Bible study goal, and Scripture memory goals. I put Scripture with the goals that I pray back to God in the personal section of my notebook.

Every other year, I read the Bible through, using various translations. On the alternate years, I focus on certain books, looking for certain threads. For example, I might study the Psalms, writing down what God is like, or Paul's writings, examining what God wants for the church.

A consistent devotional life helps me stay connected to the Source. It provides inner peace when turmoil is without. It brings me back to God's ways after I have tried my own and failed. It is an opportunity to get instructions from my Master about the day, and to bring family, friends, church, and missions to the Lord in intercession.

Jeanne Seaborn has four children, fourteen grandchildren, and one great-grandchild. She and her husband, Miles, served the Lord as missionaries in the Philippines before returning to the States, where Miles pastored a church for twenty-nine years until his retirement in 1997.

NOTES

1. William Gurnall, *Gleanings from William Gurnall*, comp. Hamilton Smith (Morgan, Pa.: Soli Deo Gloria, 1996), 104.
2. S. D. Gordon, *Quiet Talks on Prayer* (New York: Grosset & Dunlap, 1941), 15, 31, 33, 35.
3. Andrew Bonar, *Heavenly Springs* (Carlisle, Pa.: Banner of Truth, 1986), 191.
4. Ibid., 167.

PART SIX

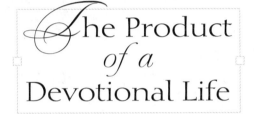

The Product
of a
Devotional Life

Let my beloved come into his garden and eat his pleasant fruits.

SONG OF SOLOMON 4:16 KJV

Like a watered garden,
Full of fragrance rare,
Ling'ring in Thy presence,
Let my life appear.

E. MAY GRIMES

CHAPTER 12

Cultivating the Garden of the Heart

Of all the human relationships Jesus had while on this earth, the one He shared with Mary of Bethany stands out as being one of the most intimate. When we first meet Mary, she is in her home, sitting at Jesus' feet, waiting quietly in His presence (Luke 10:38–42). Sometime later, when Jesus arrives in Bethany just after her brother's death, we find Mary clinging to His feet, weeping over the enormous loss she has just experienced (John 11:32–33). When we encounter Mary again, she is once more at the feet of Jesus, this time worshiping the One she has come to know, trust, and adore (John 12:1–8).

Oblivious to the curious stares and irate mumbling of the onlookers, Mary pours out her love and devotion in a costly act of worship. No one who was present that day could escape the impact of this woman's deed.

Matthew's account tells us that the disciples "were indignant. 'Why this waste?' they asked" (Matthew 26:8). To those men, Mary's act seemed extravagant, for they did not understand the infinite worth of worship. On the other hand, Jesus, who was the object of Mary's devotion, was pleased. "She has done a beautiful thing to me," he responded to the bothered disciples (v. 10). Mary's worship also had an unintended effect on herself. As she anointed Jesus' feet with the precious ointment and then wiped His feet with her hair, she became fragrant with the very perfume she had lavished on Him. Further, John tells us that "the house was filled with the fragrance of the perfume" (John 12:3).

When you and I sit at Jesus' feet and listen to His Word and then sit at His feet and lavish our worship and love upon Him, there will be an impact. Some who do not understand the nature of an intimate relationship with the Lord Jesus may object that we are being "wasteful" or fanatical by spending extended time alone in His presence, pouring out our love and devotion to Him.

Regardless of the reaction of others, one thing is certain: True worship and devotion will make our lives fragrant and will perfume the environment around us. Our homes, our churches, even our places of work will bear the sweet scent of our devotion. Most importantly, the Lord Jesus will be pleased. And ultimately that is all that really matters.

The Fragrance of Devotion

The product of a daily devotional life will bear fruit in our own lives, as we experience an ever-deepening *intimacy with the Father*. Sadly, many believers never enter into the joys and fullness of this life of oneness with the Father.

The Old Testament Jews were redeemed by God out of Egypt. They were His treasured possession. God spoke to them, but they always had to keep a safe distance, not daring to go near the mountain lest they should die from the glory of His presence. On one occasion, God invited Moses and Aaron and Nadab and Abihu, along with seventy elders of Israel, to come up the mountain to "worship at a distance" (Exodus 24:1). The Scripture says that those few chosen men "saw God, and they ate and drank" (Exodus 24:11). Together, they partook of a covenant meal, foreshadowing the Lord's Supper that New Testament believers would share with the Lord Jesus. However, Moses enjoyed an intimacy with God that was not experienced by anyone else. To Moses alone was granted the privilege of approaching the Lord and speaking with Him "face to face, as a man speaks with his friend" (Exodus 33:11).

In the New Testament, Jesus selected twelve men to be with Him, learn from Him, and walk with Him. All of these men saw the same miracles, listened to the same messages, shared in the same experiences with the Master. But three of them—Peter, James, and John—formed an "inner circle"; their friendship with Jesus went a level deeper than the others. Of those three, John the Beloved leaned on Jesus' breast and enjoyed an intimacy with Jesus that surpassed that of all others.

Those who are willing to come apart from the clamor and demands of each day's activity in order to sit at the feet of Jesus and listen to His heart are the ones who will be blessed with intimacy beyond that which most believers will ever know. It is there, in that quiet time and place, that

> He walks with me, and He talks with me,
>   And He tells me I am His own;
> And the joy we share as we tarry there
>   None other has ever known.
> —C. AUSTIN MILES (1868–1946)

The fruit of a devotional life will also be manifested in *an ordered, peaceful life*. On the survey we conducted on this topic, we asked women, "What are the benefits and blessings you have experienced as a result of your devotional life?" By far, the most frequent response (listed by 36 percent of the women) was "peace." S. D. Gordon said,

Prayer wonderfully clears the vision; steadies the nerves; defines duty; stiffens the purpose; sweetens and strengthens the spirit.[1]

Last week I received a call from the leader of a large Christian organization—an older man of God whose walk I greatly respect. He has always been a busy man; but, by his own testimony, in the past decade he has been led to place a much higher priority on his personal devotional life. When I shared with him that I was writing this book, he said this to me:

> Without any question, these past ten years, since I have been disciplined in this area, have been the greatest, the most fruitful, and the most peaceful years of my life. There has been the sense of God orchestrating my days and of the oil of the Spirit in the machinery of my life since I began to spend unhurried time with the Lord.

Time spent alone with Jesus each day will order our hearts and grant a sense of direction, enabling us to live purposeful, useful lives, directed by the power of the Holy Spirit, rather than being driven by the expectations and demands of others.

One writer described the sweet aroma he observed in his mother's life as coming from the time she spent daily with the Lord:

> My mother's habit was every day, immediately after breakfast, to withdraw for an hour to her own room, and to spend that hour in reading the Bible, in meditation and prayer. From that hour, as from a pure fountain, she drew the strength and sweetness which enabled her to fulfill all her duties, and to remain unruffled by the worries and pettinesses which are so often the trial of narrow neighborhoods.
>
> As I think of her life, and all it had to bear, I see the absolute triumph of Christian grace in the lovely ideal of a Christian lady. I never saw her temper disturbed; I never heard her speak one word of anger . . . or of idle gossip; I never observed in her any sign of a single sentiment unbecoming to a soul which had drunk of the river of the water of life, and which had fed upon manna in the barren wilderness.[2]

In his book *How to Worship Jesus Christ*, Joseph Carroll tells of another mother whose spirit was made fragrant by her life of devotion and communion with the Lord Jesus:

> I have lived in literally scores of homes in the forty years of my ministry. On one occasion, I lived in the home of a woman who had seven children and a very unsympathetic husband. She had lost two other children at birth. Though she had a large home to care for and attended the family business in her spare time, I never saw her disturbed once. There was always the fragrance of Christ about her life, and I marveled at it.
>
> While staying in her home during a conference, one morning about five o'clock I noticed light filtering in past the door; so I opened it very quietly and saw this woman kneeling by her piano. I quietly closed the door. The next morning the same thing happened, and the next morning the same thing again.
>
> So, I asked her, "What time do you rise to seek the Lord?"
>
> She replied, "Oh, that is not my decision. I made a choice long ago that when He wanted to have fellowship with me I was available. There are times when He calls me at five; there are times when He calls me at six. And on occasion, He will call about two o'clock in the morning, I think, just to test me."
>
> Always she would get up, go to her piano stool, and worship her Lord.
>
> I asked, "How long do you stay?"
>
> "Oh, that is up to Him. When He tells me to go back to bed, I go back. If He doesn't want me to sleep, I simply stay up."
>
> She was the epitome of serenity. She had made a choice, a choice that was not easy for her to make, for God had to take an idol out of her life before she made it; but when He took that idol, she was Christ's and Christ's alone.[3]

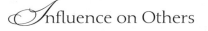

Influence on Others

As was true of both these mothers, those who spend much time alone with Jesus have a profound *influence on others* (though they themselves are seldom conscious of that influence). You may have thought that if you were to spend quality time each day with the Lord, you would not have time to meet the needs of your family and others. To the contrary, those who have been much with God touch others' lives with the power and glory of God.

After Moses had been with God, his face radiated the reflected glory of God (Exodus 34:29) and the Israelites were moved to worship (33:7–11). Do your countenance and spirit reveal the glory of God to your family and acquaintances and move them to worship God?

Isaiah 50:4–5 suggests that those whose ears are open to listen to God will have an "instructed tongue, to know the word that sustains the weary." When people are emotionally or spiritually drained, do they know that they can come to you and expect to receive wise, encouraging words from the Lord to refresh their spirit?

The Gospels indicate that Jesus' effectiveness at ministering to the needs of others was born out of His times of communion with His Father:

> *Jesus often withdrew to lonely places and prayed . . . . And the power of the Lord was present for him to heal the sick.* (LUKE 5:16–17)

In fact, whenever Jesus withdrew from the crowds for a season to pray, the crowds were drawn to Him like a magnet, for they saw in Him the likeness of His Father:

> *He went up on a mountainside to pray. . . . They ran throughout that whole region and carried the sick on mats to wherever they heard he was. . . . and all who touched him were healed.* (MARK 6:46, 55–56)

Are needy people drawn to you, as they were to Jesus, and when they come, does the power of the Holy Spirit flow through you to meet those needs?

Nowhere will the influence of intimate communion with God be more keenly felt than in our own homes and among those who know us best. The following testimony was written by the husband of one of my prayer partners. It illustrates the powerful way in which the fragrance of a woman's walk with

God can draw her family to hunger for a more intimate relationship with the Lord:

> One of my friends sometimes teases me by reminding me that I married "way over my head." I do have to admit that I often wonder why God would bless me by giving me the mate that He did. My wife is kind, fun-loving, hospitable, and generous. She doesn't grumble about what we don't have and expresses genuine appreciation for what we do.
>
> There is one thing, however, that stands head and shoulders above all her precious qualities—she walks intimately with God. I'm not referring to a kind of heavenly stupor; I mean that she simply obeys God. She listens to what He says, and then she does it. That's not to say that she doesn't struggle, but when she does, she doesn't blame her circumstances or become moody. She asks God to search her heart, and she waits for His answer.
>
> I, on the other hand, have often resisted God, languishing in stubbornness, rebellion, and pride. And I'm not fully out of their grip yet. But my life did begin to change a few years ago. Much of that change, my turning to God, came as the result of my wife's consistent, faithful example of godliness.
>
> There is a reason for my wife being the kind of Christian that she is. One of the landmarks that she points to in her life is a time when, during a week of summer youth camp, the speaker encouraged everyone to commit to read their Bible every day for one year. To her, a commitment was a commitment; if she made the promise she was bound by her word to keep it. So when she made that commitment before God to read her Bible every day for a year, she meant business.
>
> My wife was in junior high school then. As I write this testimony, we have been married for nearly sixteen years, and I have never known her to miss a single day in having her quiet time. Not one.
>
> I'm not saying these things to put my wife on a pedestal. My point is that faithfully taking a few minutes out of each day to meet alone with God in His Word and prayer has formed her into a godly woman. It is her life that "won" me (1 Peter 3:1). If she had nagged me about certain things, or manipulated, or ridiculed, she would only have succeeded in driving me away from wanting to grow in Christ. Instead, she lived a very real life of simple faith and devotion to Christ. And it made me thirsty for what she had.

We have children now. By God's grace they are growing up with an understanding that having personal devotions is a normal part of the daily routine. The older ones have already begun to have their own quiet time. Much like my wife's example to me, we didn't instruct or require this of our children. They've simply seen Mommy and Daddy reading their Bibles and praying, and they want to do the same.

God's Word has been like a medicine to reduce my anger, worry, and impatience. It has acted as a map in helping our family make decisions or reroute our ill-advised plans. It has provided light to reveal snares that were sometimes hiding in the shadows. God's Word has become for us a thing we simply could not do without.

I thank God for a youth speaker who encouraged a group of junior-high campers to read their Bibles. And I thank God for a young lady who made that commitment and kept it. I can't describe what a blessing it is to be married to a woman who lives and thinks biblically. When we are discussing any issue, whether a hard or not-so-difficult one, I know I'm talking to a lady who has been with Jesus! That means a lot to this husband!

From Barrenness to Beauty

Several years ago, I built my first home. When I purchased the wooded lot, it was covered with tall pine trees as well as lots of brush, tall grass, and weeds. The property was beautifully situated overlooking a river, but, for all practical purposes, it was useless. I remember when the heavy earthmoving equipment rolled in to clear the land. Many of those trees were cut down to make room for the house. The brush was all cleared out, the land was leveled, and the builder began to dig a hole for the basement. The dirt all around that hole quickly got packed down by construction equipment, leaving ground that was hard, dry, and not particularly attractive.

Once the house was up, a landscape architect met with me to propose a plan for the property. He showed me drawings of what he had in mind—lots of trees, plants, shrubs, and ground cover. I couldn't begin to picture what he saw in his mind's eye—I didn't know a hosta from a hydrangea. Somewhat apprehensively, I signed a contract and said, "OK, let's do it!"

That fall, I paid the landscaping company what seemed to me like a fortune, and then sat back to watch. I couldn't believe my eyes! The plants they brought in were tiny, scrawny, and unimpressive, to say the least. Grass seed was planted, but I couldn't see a single blade of grass, much less the verdant carpet I had anticipated. More than once, I said to myself, "I paid that much money for *this*?" I had envisioned looking out my window at a lush, colorful visual feast. Instead, there was no color; there was no beauty; and there were large bare spots with no plants at all.

Sensing my lack of enthusiasm, the landscaper urged me to "just wait and see," assuring me that in time I would be pleased with the results. I waited, and I waited, and I waited. When the first Michigan winter hit, things looked even worse. The trees were bare, the ground was bare, and the shrubs looked like sticks poking out of the ground.

The next spring, a few trees and shrubs produced nice blossoms. The grass finally looked like grass. But the overall scene was still less than spectacular. And the weeds—oh, the weeds! I had no idea how omnipresent and persistent they could be! I certainly wasn't getting much enjoyment out of this "garden."

I waited some more. We pulled more weeds and applied fertilizer to the beds, and kept waiting. Each year, a gardener pruned back the plants, shrubs, and trees. That didn't exactly look like progress to me.

But what I could not see was that the sunshine, the rain, the fertilizer, the pruning, even the heavy winter snows, were all helping those plants to get bigger and stronger and to spread their roots deep into the soil. Slowly but surely, the ground cover began to take root and spread. Each spring I could see the evidence of new growth at the ends of those evergreen branches. In and among the original plantings, we planted hundreds of daffodil bulbs and lots of brightly colored annuals.

It has now been over six years. Now I can step outdoors any time between April and October and see an array of beautiful flowers and plants. The daffodils come up first—what a splendid picture they make. By the time they are gone, there are azaleas, astilbes, and chrysanthemums to replace them, followed by splendid daylilies and foxglove, with wild strawberries poking up through the ground cover. What a delight to see butterflies, hummingbirds, cardinals, bluebirds, squirrels, bunnies, and deer making their home in this paradise.

This outdoor refuge did not spring up overnight. And it did not just "happen." It is the fruit of years of planning, investment, effort, and cultivation, coupled with God's watchful, wise care and provision. Like all gardens, this garden requires continual maintenance and care—always keeping an eye out for the disease, rot, moles, and weeds that tend to creep in and take over.

After years of careful oversight, my garden is now fulfilling the purpose for which it was intended. It is a thing of great beauty and provides enjoyment and pleasure to all who visit. It is a peaceful, joyous haven, fragrant, full of new surprises, ever-changing—a place where hearts are gladdened and lifted toward the Creator.

My Life—A Garden for Him

In the first section of this book, we were introduced to the Shulammite bride of the Song of Solomon. You recall that the king in that amazing love story does not select his bride from among the most eligible women of the capital city; rather, he chooses a plain, ordinary country girl who is "burned out" from working in her family's vineyard. He takes her back to the palace and invites her to come into his chamber (Song of Solomon 1:4). In that intimate, quiet place, he lavishes his love upon her. As she partakes of his fruit, she is restored:

I sat down under his shadow with great delight, and his fruit was sweet to my taste. He brought me to the banqueting house, and his banner over me was love. (SONG OF SOLOMON 2:3–4 KJV)

The Song of Solomon is the story of the growing intimacy shared by the royal couple. It is the story of the cultivation of a pure, rich love—the intertwining of two lives to become one. As the bride receives the tender words and touch of her Beloved, and as she responds to his initiative, she is transformed—transformed by grace, transformed by love.

The once common peasant girl becomes a lovely, gracious queen. The girl who was once tired of living now has a purpose for living. The young woman who once resented having to work in the vineyard is now eager to go out into the vineyard and serve with her Beloved (7:11–12). The woman who was once a nobody now brings joy and fullness to the other women of the city, as she introduces them to her Beloved.

This transformation does not just happen—it takes place in the context of a relationship—a relationship that requires constant attention and care. But there is an ultimate purpose that makes all the investment of time and effort worthwhile. What is that purpose? To bring delight and pleasure to the Beloved.

As their love matures, the Beloved likens his bride's heart to a garden—a trysting place where he finds great joy and satisfaction. He describes the paradise that he finds in that exclusive place set apart for him:

A garden inclosed is my sister, my spouse; a spring shut up, a fountain sealed. Thy plants are an orchard of pomegranates, with pleasant fruits; . . . a fountain of gardens, a well of living waters, and streams from Lebanon. (SONG OF SOLOMON 4:12–13, 15 KJV)

The bride responds by affirming that her sole desire is that her garden would bring pleasure to her Beloved. She welcomes whatever is required—the cold, biting north winds or the warm, balmy south winds—to cultivate a place of beauty, fragrance, and delight for him:

> *Awake, O north wind; and come, thou south; blow upon my garden, that the spices thereof may flow out. Let my beloved come into his garden, and eat his pleasant fruits.* (SONG OF SOLOMON 4:16 KJV)

The garden that was once "hers" is now his. The fragrance of that garden is for Him. All the fruit of the garden is His. All that she is and all that she has is His. It is all for Him, "for thou hast created all things, and for thy pleasure they are and were created" (Revelation 4:11 KJV).

And so, dear one, your Beloved, the One who has chosen and redeemed you to be His own, longs to find refuge and delight in the garden of your heart. As you walk in union and communion with Him, a sweet fragrance will be released and luscious fruit will be born—the fragrance and the fruit of His Spirit. You will be blessed; others will be blessed. And it is all, all, all for the Beloved.

MAKING IT PERSONAL

1. Write a love letter to Jesus. Thank Him for how He brought you to Himself and the difference His love has made in your life. Express to Him your desire for your life to be a "garden" that brings pleasure to Him.

2. Take time to think through and record two or three of the most important things God has taught you through your reading of this book. (You may wish to refresh your memory by paging back through the book or reviewing the "Making It Personal" sections.)

3. Go back and review your answer to the first question on page 30. How has the quality of your personal devotional life changed since you began reading this book?

   What further changes would you like to see take place in your devotional life in the days ahead?

4. If you have not already done so, *will you make a commitment, beginning today, to spend some time alone with God every day, listening and responding to His Word?* Record your commitment in your journal. Pray and ask God to grant the desire and the grace to choose with Mary that "one thing that is needful."

FROM THE HEART OF
Joni Eareckson Tada

As the hymn says, "In the rustling grass I hear Him pass, He speaks to me everywhere."[4] For the Christian who has thrown open her heart wide to the wonders of God, this is a way of living. God speaks everywhere. God is intentional and infuses purpose and meaning in everything around us. Such communion with God is always serendipitous and full of surprises. It's a wonderful thing to see God in everything.

I generally enjoy meeting God every place. But I specifically meet Him in a certain place. This is how I view a quiet time—it's a smaller, slightly more structured slice of a larger and more broadly beautiful experience with Him. In other words, a quiet time, for me, is not a boxed-in, compartmentalized fifteen minutes that I block in on mornings or evenings and then hopefully have it influence the rest of my day. Rather, it's simply a period of time in a larger continuum of communion with the Lord Jesus. And all of it comprises a "way of living."

Earlier, I used the word "structure" to describe my quiet time. The ingredients for a good quiet time always involve Bible reading and meditation as well as prayer which highlights those meditations. It's also a time of silent soul surrender and waiting on the Lord. Listening and watching. For although it is true He speaks to us "everywhere," it is also true that He has certain and specific things to say which require our undivided attention fostered through silence and stillness.

To carry over insights gleaned from a quiet time, a good closing prayer is, "Lord, tell me more about this during the rest of the day, would You?" Invariably, He does.

Joni Eareckson Tada is an artist, author, and the founder of JAF Ministries, an organization that accelerates Christian ministry in the disability community. Joni and her husband, Ken, have been married over eighteen years and make their home in Southern California.

NOTES

PART PAGE: "Speak, Lord, in the Stillness," lyrics by E. May Grimes, setting by Alfred B. Smith. Copyright 1951 Singspiration Music/ASCAP. All rights reserved. Reprinted by special permission of Brentwood-Benson Music Publishing, Inc.

1. S. D. Gordon, *Quiet Talks on Prayer* (New York: Grosset and Dunlap, 1941), 214.

2. Farrar, in *Streams in the Desert*, vol. 1, comp. Mrs. Charles E. Cowman (Cowman, 1925; Grand Rapids: Zondervan, c. 1965–66), reading for September 13.

3. Joseph S. Carroll, *How to Worship Jesus Christ* (Chicago: Moody, 1991), 27–28.

4. Maltbe D. Babcock; "This Is My Father's World"; from "Thoughts for Every Day Living" (New York: Scribner's, 1901; copyright 1929, Katharine T. Babcock).

APPENDIX

RECOMMENDED DEVOTIONAL BOOKS

Arnold, Duane W. H., comp. and trans. *Prayers of the Martyrs.* Grand Rapids: Zondervan, 1991.

Bennett, Arthur, ed. *The Valley of Vision.* Carlisle, Pa.: Banner of Truth Trust, 1975.

Bonar, Andrew A. *Heavenly Springs.* Carlisle, Pa.: Banner of Truth, 1986.

Cowman, Mrs. Charles E., comp. *Streams in the Desert.* Vol. 1. Cowman Publications, 1925; Grand Rapids: Zondervan, c. 1965–66.

Elliot, Elisabeth. *Keep a Quiet Heart.* Ann Arbor: Vine, 1995.

_____. *A Lamp for My Feet.* Ann Arbor: Vine, 1985.

Fenelon, François. *The Seeking Heart.* Sargent, Ga.: SeedSowers Christian Books, 1992.

Gurnall, William. *The Christian in Complete Armour.* Chicago: Moody, 1994.

_____. *Gleanings from William Gurnall.* Edited by Hamilton Smith. Morgan, Pa.: Soli Deo Gloria, 1996.

Rekindling the Inner Fire series. Edited by David Hazard. A series of devotional books, each based on a well-known figure or group: Augustine, Bernard of Clairvaux, Amy Carmichael, Francis of Assisi, Julian of Norwich, John of the Cross, Andrew Murray, Hannah W. Smith, Theresa of Avila, and some early disciples (Barnabas, Ignatius, Polycarp, Clement). Minneapolis: Bethany House.

Smith, Hannah Whitall. *God Is Enough.* Edited by Melvin E. Dieter and Hallie A. Dieter. Grand Rapids: Asbury, 1986.

Tozer, A. W. *The Christian Book of Mystical Verse.* Camp Hill, Pa.: Christian Publications, 1963.

Watson, Thomas. *Gleanings from Thomas Watson.* Edited by Hamilton Smith. Morgan, Pa.: Soli Deo Gloria, 1995.

Companion Guide to *A Place of Quiet Rest* by Nancy Leigh DeMoss

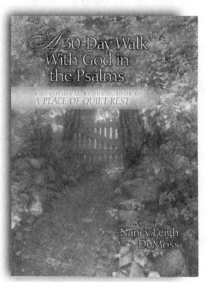

ISBN: 978-0-8024-6644-0

Would you like to develop a meaningful daily quiet time?
A 30-Day Walk with God in the Psalms will help get you started

Without a doubt, one of the most significant influences in the life of Nancy Leigh DeMoss was the example of parents who practiced the spiritual discipline of a daily devotional life. For Nancy, the habit of setting time aside alone with the Lord each day has become nothing less than a necessity —a key to cultivating intimacy with God. And to the degree you make this your daily focus, you too will experience great freedom, joy and blessing in the Lord.

A 30-Day Walk with God in the Psalms is a companion to the best-selling *A Place of Quiet Rest* but can be used by anyone, at any time, to draw you closer to your Heavenly Father. Reading, studying, memorizing, meditating on, and praying through the Psalms will help tutor you in a lifestyle of praise and worship.

MOODY
Publishers™

From the Word to Life
1-800-678-6928 www.MoodyPublishers.com

The Revive Our Hearts Series

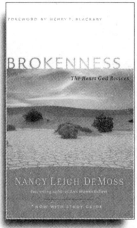

ISBN: 978-0-8024-1281-2

Brokenness
The Heart God Revives

Do you need a fresh infusion of the
Grace of God in your life?

Brokenness is an invitation to encounter God in a
whole new way. It is a call to discover His heart and
His ways; a challenge to embrace a radically new way
of thinking and living, in which the way up is down,
death brings life, and brokenness is the pathway to
wholeness.

Surrender
The Heart God Controls

In her second powerful and important book in the
Revive Our Hearts Series, Nancy Leigh DeMoss
considers the meaning of Christian surrender.
She makes a compelling case for choosing the
pathway of unconditional surrender to God.
For it is only through a surrendered life that we
will receive a host of blessings that cannot be
experienced any other way.

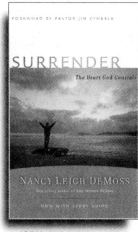

ISBN: 978-0-8024-1280-5

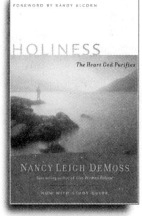

ISBN: 978-0-8024-1279-9

Holiness
The Heart God Purifies

Nancy Leigh DeMoss teaches that we must make it our
constant, conscious ambition and aim to be holy. Just
as an athlete sets his sight on winning an Olympic gold
medal, so we as believers must focus on the pursuit of
holiness. And the reward that awaits us brings a depth
of joy that far outweighs a fading gold medal—the
humble pleasure of hearing the Father say, "Well done,
good and faithful servant."

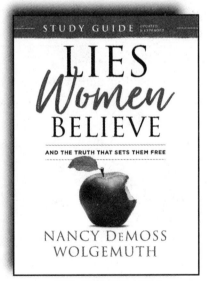

More Titles from Nancy Leigh DeMoss

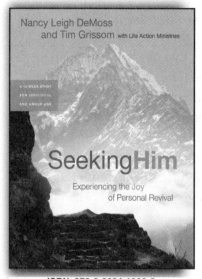

ISBN: 978-0-8024-1362-8

Seeking Him
Experiencing the Joy of
Personal Revival

With Tim Grissom

Revival is not just an emotional touch . . .
but a complete transformation! It can happen . . . in your heart . . . in your home . . . in
your church . . . in your world.

Seeking Him is a 12-week interactive study
on personal revival.

DVD Available: **978-0-8024-1367-3**

Choosing Forgiveness
Your Journey to Freedom

God forgiving as we do? That's a scary
thought. Leading author and radio host
Nancy Leigh DeMoss explains how
forgiving like God is a choice that frees us
from the burdens of bitterness, anger, and
isolation. Women and men struggling with
long-held hurts will be called to repentance
and ultimately to the healing power of
forgivenss.

ISBN: 978-0-8024-3253-7

MOODY
Publishers™

From the Word to Life
1-800-678-6928 www.MoodyPublishers.com